ROMEO SOZZI
& PROMEMORIA

ROMEO SOZZI & PROMEMORIA

THE DESIGNER BEHIND
THE MOST BEAUTIFUL FURNITURE
IN THE WORLD

edited by
Pierre Léonforte

Rizzoli
NEW YORK

New York Paris London Milan

CONTENTS

PREFACE
BY JOSÉ CARRERAS

I often meet up with Romeo, and I'm always glad to do so—in Austria, in London, at the Scala. Music, of which he is a refined and knowledgeable admirer, is not the only interest that brings us together. Our friendship is fueled by the sharing of many passions but, generally speaking, by a vision that embraces all the dimensions of life.

Even before being a successful designer, Romeo is an artist. I don't know if I admire more his exquisitely beautiful creations, in which he infuses all his talent and his eye for detail, or the passion and the inexhaustible energy with which he brings them to life.

His nature as an artist is also revealed in the way he charms those who meet him with his smile and his charisma; in his bubbly, contagious enthusiasm for what he loves and, in between, in the nuances of his sensibility.

We are joined by the understanding and the complicity of those who look to the equilibriums of life in the same way: Romeo is an indefatigable worker who, alongside his relentless search for inspiration and ideas in art, in culture, and in nature, also knows how to make room for the pleasures of conviviality.

Of all our meetings, I preserve the indelible memory of a September day in Varenna, when we savored our reciprocal company as we talked of music, art, life, of great and simple things at the same time, with the colors of the garden and the blue of the lake in the background. I am certain that the same memory resounds in his mind with the same intensity.

THE HOUSE ON THE LAKE

The invitation, handwritten and personally signed on a silver-edged card, was quite specific, and a bit mysterious: *I am expecting you at my house in Varenna. Access via the lake recommended.* Specific yet mysterious, indicating Sozzi's intention to do everything possible to amaze his guests. It was a safe bet that Sozzi had once again dreamed up a marvelous surprise for his friends from all over the world—his house in Varenna on Lake Como offers a perfect setting for the festivities that he loves.

No need for maps, compasses, or GPS: Varenna is right there, on the banks of **Lake Como.** And no need for the *traghetti* that ferry passengers between Como, Bellagio, and other local attractions. Sozzi has sent his own boat to Como: a **Riva** *motoscafo* Tritone, a veritable floating jewel, which he will tell us later is the best-looking Riva of all, styled like a fine piece of furniture, as beautiful as a Ruhlmann desk. Once on board, the motor warms up and we head for Varenna, with a few slight swerves and dodges along the way, amiably allowed by a skipper who knows this lake—which is rumored to be one of the deepest in Europe—by heart. Lake Como is a true, small inland sea. On these shores Lombard families built villas and palaces, and later stopped coming, sometimes forgetting their properties entirely. Lake Como owes its present-day beauty to this neglect. But it has not been disfigured—everything, down to the tiniest azalea petal, has been preserved. Intensely romantic, it has inspired Pliny the Younger, Mary Shelley, Byron, Goethe, Ibsen, Mark Twain, Petrarch, and Hermann Hesse. It is evoked by August Strindberg's *Miss Julie* and by Stendhal, who described its rugged wooded landscape in the first chapter of *The Charterhouse of Parma*. Since the Renaissance, Lake Como has been an earthly vestige of paradise lost, with a charm that instantly assuages the effects of Milan.

On either side of the dark, nearly black water—so calm that it seems barely disturbed by the wakes produced by boats headed in every direction—the shores rise abruptly, luxuriant with Alpine, Mediterranean, and tropical plants. Lined with villages and elegant, patrician houses—some made more enchanting by encroaching ruin and haunted, one could easily imagine, by the ghosts of Isadora Duncan

[p. 16] ⟶

◆ LAKE COMO, A TRUE INLAND SEA

Scanned from east to west on a map of northern Italy, the country's famous lakes seem to spell out a coded message. Garda and Iseo, Como and Lugano, and then Maggiore. All of them either lie within or border the Lombardy region—hence its nickname, "Land of the Lakes." Lake Como, also called Lario, is a double lake with twin roots: Como to the west and Lecco to the east, with the headland of Bellagio marking the divide. With its upside-down "Y" shape, Lake Como resembles a divining rod wielded by an Alpine giant standing in St. Moritz. Spanning 56 square miles at an altitude of 650 feet, 28 miles in length with 87 miles of shoreline, Lake Como is reputed for its exceptional depth of 1,345 feet. The lake has spawned a thousand legends, including the tale of Mussolini's lost treasure—supposedly now buried under so much silt that no one could ever hope to retrieve it. The lake's waters are plied by a variety of commercial watercraft—*traghetti*, ferries, and paddle wheelers, all descendants of the steamboats of the nineteenth century, connecting the larger towns and certain resorts with the consistency of a Swiss watch—as well as a swarm of light private craft, including rowboats, motorboats, fishing boats, speedboats, dinghies, and sailboats of every size, for both sport and transport. Most of the locals own a boat, with the exception of the VIPs, who arrive by helicopter or seaplane.

Who still remembers the lake's historic watercraft, the gondolas, genuine floating carriages with no relation to the Venetian version, or the *comballi* with their sails and flat bottoms? Now they are nothing but nautical memories in black and white.

More lasting are the five winds that blow hot and cold across the water: the northwesterly Tivano, which rises in the morning and whose absence heralds bad weather; the southerly Breva; the Alpine Vento that precedes the snows; the Montivo, a continental breeze that cools the summer evenings; and the Menaggino, the eponymous wind which blows in strong gusts from the nearby valley—violently enough to raise high waves that ripple across the lake's surface.

◆ RIVA, THE ULTIMATE MOTORBOAT

A mahogany hull with twenty-four coats of varnish, gleaming chrome trim, a cinemascope windshield ... Pietro Riva's first launches took to the water in 1842 in Sarnico, on the shores of Lake Iseo in Lombardy. Ever since, they have been cutting a high profile in the prestigious wake of the famous Rivarama, Ariston, Aquarama, and Sunriva, the very definition of "emblematic models." But every Riva is a floating Rolls Royce, firmly anchoring the brand in the nautical traditions of the rich and famous—everybody who is anybody has piloted, owned, or sold a Riva at one time or another. The boats are still manufactured on the shores of Lake Iseo, where the workshop for new models adjoins the one for restoring vintage Rivas, which command an even bigger market.

The Bugatti of the blue, a masterpiece of nautical carpentry, the Riva Tritone was designed by Carlo Riva in 1950. The brand's very first twin-engine boat, the prototype was completed in two months for Prince Antonio Amato di Caserta and delivered personally by Carlo Riva. Its maiden voyage on a very choppy sea between Capri and Naples gave the engines a tough workout, proving the craft's reliability. The next three Tritones were soon ordered, respectively, by the Hollywood B-movie and TV producer Roland Reed (who gave the world *Space Ranger*, *Buck Rogers*, and *Captain Video*), the Italian winemaker Fazi Battaglia, and Count Mario Augusta, future president of the Federazione Motonautica. Other customers for the Tritone, which in the meantime had set a speed record of 80 kph (50 mph), included Prince Giovanni Pignatelli di Monteroduni and Prince Rainer of Monaco, who gave one as a gift to Princess Grace in 1958. Between 1952 and 1966, the Tritone was the flagship of the Riva boatyards, whose production doubled during that period. Sculpted from stem to stern, with its covered cabin in-between, by the power of waterborne legend, the Tritone was succeeded by the Aquarama. Quickly nicknamed the "Ferrari of the Seas," it is a treasured collector's item today. The exquisite woodwork that gives the Rivas' superstructure their premium aesthetic quite naturally inspired a creation by Romeo Sozzi: a variation of his *Battista* folding table, given the aquatic name *Lotus*.

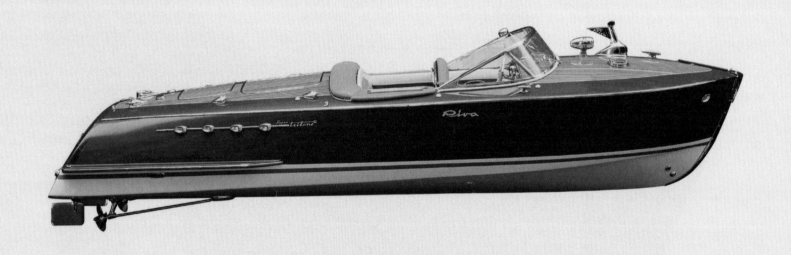

THE RIVA TRITONE

facts and figures

…

Type: runabout

Years produced: 1950-1967

Number of models built: 258

Overall length: 25–27 feet (Super)

Maximum width: 8.26 feet

Maximum capacity: 8 people

Engines: 2 Chris Craft or 2 Chrysler

Maximum HP: 2 × 290 (Chrysler)

Maximum speed: 52 mph

or Gabriele d'Annunzio—both shores exude an inexpressible sense of tranquility and well-being. Each village shares a specific character. Along the western side we admire, both near and far, dozens of villas and private parks dating from the late seventeenth century, including the famous Villa Carlotta, Villa La Gaeta—where the 2006 James Bond film *Casino Royale* was shot—and Villa del Balbianello, surrounded by an extraordinary rock garden that seems to have been groomed with tweezers. This spectacular property has provided the setting for a host of films, including *A Month by the Lake* with Vanessa Redgrave, Uma Thurman, and Alida Valli (1995), and *Star Wars II, Attack of the Clones* (2002). Built in the late eighteenth century on the ruins of a Franciscan monastery, which was the residence of several cardinals as well as the aristocratic anti-Austrian patriot Count Luigi Porro Lambertenghi, the villa stood empty for forty years until the end of World War I, when the American general Butler Ames purchased it and oversaw its restoration. Its last owner was Count Guido Monzino, who bequeathed the property, along with his collections and archives, to the FAI (Fondo per l'Ambiente Italiano) in 1988. Famous for funding and organizing major Arctic expeditions and an ascent of Mount Everest in 1973, the count was laid to rest in the estate's former icehouse. His story alone sums up the evocative narrative power of the lakeshore, a crossroads of extraordinary lives. The story overlaps tales from other villas, such as the sublime hotel Villa d'Este, or the holiday homes of George Clooney and Richard Branson, who are more interesting to celebrity-spotting tourists.

On the eastern shore the style is less English and more Italian, with a touch of French. Where Lake Como meets Lake Lecco (the southeastern branch) at the tip of a hilly spur of land, stands the headland-village of Bellagio, an architectural bowsprit entirely protected as a cultural monument. Bellagio is a site, a spirit, and perhaps also the spiritual seat of the lakes, even though until a quarter of a century ago its inhabitants matter-of-factly chose the local priest by popular ballot. Bellagio is also world-renowned for the Grand Hotel Villa Serbelloni, a palatial five-star establishment right on the lakeshore, which is one of the most beautiful places on earth. From Bellagio, Varenna is clearly visible on the horizon. Nestled into the landscape as though posing for a postcard, Varenna is perfectly framed, reminiscent of the painting depicting the town painted from the lake in 1818, which is owned by the Milan's Biblioteca Nazionale Braidense.

Before arriving at its destination, the Riva makes one last detour for a glimpse

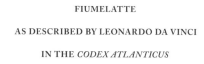

FIUMELATTE

AS DESCRIBED BY LEONARDO DA VINCI

IN THE *CODEX ATLANTICUS*

◆

1478-1519

"The Fiumelaccio (sic), which falls from a height of more than 100 braccia from the source whence it springs, perpendicularly, into the lake with an inconceivable roar and noise. This spring flows only in August and September."

of the rapidly flowing Fiumelatte, a geological curiosity so distinctive that Leonardo da Vinci described it in his *Codex Atlanticus*. It is in fact a river, one of the shortest in Italy: a 984-foot waterfall that bubbles forth from a cave and empties ten minutes down the hillside into the Lake Como. Along the way, its furious roiling creates an optical effect: its frothy water appears white as milk, making the name *Fiumelatte* "milk river" appropriate. It's also a playful river, disappearing in the fall and only coming out of hiding when the snow melts in the spring. The boat halts for a moment at its mouth to let us feel the intense cooling effect of its enveloping mist. Fiumelatte is also the name of the hamlet that straddles this short stretch of river, a tiny town described by the poet and patriot Giacomo Marchini as *"a village that looks like laundry stretched out on a clothesline."* It's worth noting that designer Piero Fornasetti had a house in Fiumelatte, and that much earlier, in the late 1860s, Richard Wagner looked here for a house worthy of his beloved Cosima (the daughter of Franz Liszt), who was born in Bellagio.

On the northern arm of Lake Como, **Varenna*** is a medieval town that, starting in the early nineteenth century, became a fashionable resort for the aristocracy of Mitteleuropa, the English nobility and the grand families of Lombardy. Its well-known, part-time residents included Ferdinand I, Emperor of Austria and King of Lombardy-Venetia, his brothers and their retinues, not to mention the King of Württemberg, the Grand Duchess of Leuchtenberg, the Savoy princes, and the kings of Italy.

Its sunny weather and geographic location sheltered from the winds made Varenna a hotspot for the crowned heads and beautiful people of the era. It offered a pleasant, relaxing lifestyle, enhanced by the presence of numerous gardens—fragrant enclaves brimming with lemon and orange trees, cedars and rose bushes,

[p. 22] ⟶

VARENNA, HISTORY
OF A LAKESIDE VILLAGE

Across the water from Menaggio, 2.8 miles away at the lake's widest point, Varenna rises up 720 feet above sea level. Shielded from the winds by the mountains Grigna, Grignetta, Legnone, and Resegone, bathed in sunlight from dawn to dusk thanks to its east-west exposure which also spares it the harsh winter weather, Varenna enjoys the same mild climate as Nice. Even in January, the thermometer almost never dips below 41 degrees. The town is said to be protected from the wrath of the gods and ill winds. The people there live at a slower pace—and for a longer time.

Varenna's origins date back to the days of the Roman Empire. It was mentioned as long ago as 769, in the will of one Diacono Grato di Monza, who owned property there when it was a fortified town with, according to local lore, a war-loving population. In the early twelfth century, the inhabitants of Comacina, Lake Como's only island, took refuge in Varenna after their settlement was sacked during the war between Emperor Federico Barbarossa and Milan. All of the island's prominent families, the Serpontis, the Salas, and the Greppis, for example, established new seats in the town, which for a short period was called "Isola (or Insula) Nuova." Until 1310, when Don Carlo Borromeo reined in a scandal-ridden clergy, Varenna was placed under the authority of the Archdiocese of Milan. Then it was the Sforzas, against whom the Varennese resisted, before pledging fealty to the Viscontis, then to the tyrant Franchino Rusca, and later to Giuseppe Valeriano Sfondrati, Lord of the Riviera. Varenna then passed under Spanish, French, and Austrian rule, until, like the other lake regions, it joined the nineteenth-century Italian unification movement known as *Risorgimento*. During all this time, the easiest way to reach Varenna from the other villages was by water. This relative isolation, which served as a rampart against epidemics, was shattered in 1817 when the Stelvio road was built along the eastern shore.

The medieval arches and gates were demolished, including Porta Varenna adjoining Villa Venini, whose concave walls lined one side of this new terrestrial traffic artery as it wound its way between the existing dwellings. Spreading out from Piazza San Giorgio, which boasts nearly as many church steeples as cypress trees, the streets of the village, now a discreet, elegant lakeside resort, filled up with closely-spaced houses, gardens, and terraces interconnected by stone arches above alleyways that slip down to the shore. Celebrated in painting, song, and poetry, Varenna nurtures the artistic impulse. From an everyday perspective, in the nineteenth century the village, along with its neighbor Fiumelatte, became an active center of the marble industry. No fewer than four different varieties were extracted from the nearby quarries: *lumachella verde*, also called *serpentine*, the white/brown *lumachella grigio*, the white-speckled gray *occhiadino*, and *nero*, prized by the ancient Romans and considered by many to be the most beautiful marble of all. Paying homage to the successive generations of *marmuritt*, the Varennese marble workers, Riva dei Marmisti runs along the edge of the lake.

The water here is the purest of anywhere on Lake Como. In June the fishermen catch *missoltini*, a thin silvery fish and a feature of the local culinary heritage, pressed in wooden or metal cans with laurel leaves after drying on a line for twelve days and savored with buttered polenta. Once considered humble fare, the dish has become a precious specialty. Now accessible by road, rail, or water, Varenna has come a long way since its days of sleepy isolation.

compared by erudite visitors like Giovanni Bonanomi to the gardens of Sappho. For many years the epicenter of Varennese social life was the Royal Victoria, a luxury hotel. In its day the hotel welcomed the cream of society, from Queen Victoria, who stayed there incognito as the Countess of Clare, to Austrian general Joseph Radetzky von Radetz, and the playwright-politician Felice Cavallotti. Its gardens, designed by the architect Sir H. Inigo Triggs in 1901, also drew crowds. After all, without a garden, it's impossible to see and be seen at the lakefront.

The convergence of the world's style- and decision-makers upon Lake Como in general and Varenna in particular was closely associated with the Grand Tour, as well as the veneration of certain illustrious residents. This was the case of Lecco, the other "big" town on the lake besides Como, and home of the greatest Italian novelist of the nineteenth century, Alessandro Manzoni, who spent his entire youth there and then made an effort never to return. Lecco is also where Romeo Sozzi opened his first Promemoria showroom, now a pilgrimage site of a different kind.

With its brightly-hued walls, flying buttresses, cobblestone streets, steps, and narrow lanes leading down to the lake, Varenna bears few traces of its medieval origins as a fortified monastic outpost. What survives are its larger buildings, converted over the years into opulent residences, some now veritable palaces in the midst of fabulous gardens: Villa Isimbardi, known as Villa Cipressi, and Villa Capuana, where Wagner is said to have stayed under an assumed name. And, there is, of course, the renowned Villa Monastero, a former Cistercian convent. One of its most illustrious owners, starting in 1869, was Carolina Maumary, a German aristocrat whose sister Luisa married the Italian painter and politician Massimo d'Azeglio. The villa was later sold to German industrialist Walter Kees, and then to the philanthropist Marco De Marchi, founder of the Istituto Italiano di Idrobiologia, a branch of the National Research Council. Today Villa Monastero is the institute's headquarters, and the scene of official summit meetings that bring together luminaries of the physical sciences, many of them Nobel laureates.

Varenna was also known for its houses that became cultural salons. Like Casa Tinai, occupied by playwright and librettist Leopoldo Marenco (1831-1899), the prolific author of *Celeste*, *Saffo*, and *Il Falconiere di Pietra Ardena*. Marenco entertained the artistic elite of his day, including Amilcare Ponchielli, composer of *Dance of the Hours*, the famous musical publisher Giulio Ricordi, and the orchestral conductor Pietro Platania, director of the Conservatory of Palermo, who, in turn, invited Giuseppe Verdi. The painters Sebastiano De Albertis and Carlo Pittara were also frequent visitors. But the most habitual and free-spirited guest of all was the cellist Gaetano Braga, composer of *La Serenata: Leggenda Valacca* and *Mélodies de Varenna*, a notorious spendthrift and the protégé of Countess Luisa Campioni Venini, whose musical salon and soirées made her Varenna residence, Villa Venini, known far and wide. Today Varenna's salon happens to be the lakeside home of Romeo Sozzi, who has an endless store of tales and anecdotes about his historic property, which became his home by pure chance in 2001.

Then called Villa Mapelli and listed in the guidebooks under that name, the house had been offered for sale by the last heir of Count Ottorino Mapelli, who had bought it in 1926 as a family holiday home. A house on the lake—and an old one at that—not exactly what Sozzi was looking for. He had been dreaming of a modern glass house surrounded by nature. He only visited the house on behalf of clients, one rainy Friday during the Milan Furniture Fair, taking a close friend along for the ride.

Nothing about the house seemed likely to win him over: the fatigue of the week together with the long drive from Milan; the disadvantage of seeing the place in an unflattering light with the garden plunged into darkness; the discouraging interiors. Neither the rain-soaked Romeo Sozzi nor anyone else present expected a positive outcome. Back on the road, he and his friend crossed Villa Mapelli off their mental list and turned their attention to stopping for a pizza to lift their spirits. But after driving no more than twenty minutes, no doubt at his usual breakneck speed, Sozzi suddenly braked, turned to his friend and said, "What if we bought it ourselves?"

Clinging to the rocky shore, Villa Mapelli is one of the most elegant of Varenna's lakeside houses. It was built in 1655 for a resident of Bellano, a town further north on the same shore, but the original owner, whose name has been lost to the flow of time, sold it a few years later to the Serponti family. They in turn sold it in 1685 to another prominent Varennese family, the Stampas, who expanded the building in the early eighteenth century, adding the two symmetrical wings matching the existing neoclassical style. The house remained in their possession until 1807, when Margherita de Funk, Francesco Stampa's widow, sold it to Natale Pirelli, a member of another eminent local family and the ancestor of Leopoldo Pirelli, who would help make Italy a twentieth-century economic power through the industrial empire that bears his name.

In 1816, Veneranda Pirelli married Giovanni Battista Venini, joining another important local family, with its own coat of arms and illustrious future descendant: Jacopo Venini, founder of the prestigious Venini glassworks in Venice. Sixty years later, the couple's son and heir Giacomo Venini, a lawyer by trade, was leading an opulent life in the former Villa Pirelli, now named for his own family. He succeeded in acquiring an adjoining plot of land that had belonged to the Beata Vergine del Monastero convent, and was historically known as the Olivedo di Varenna. Much respected in the region, the lawyer married an aristocrat, Countess Luigia (Luisa Campioni), whose family had had its seat in Varenna since the fifteenth century.

Together they welcomed a string of celebrated guests to their home, including authors, poets, and musicians, and hosted frequent concerts and musical events, making a specialty of moonlight serenades, a romantic diversion for which the generous Gaetano Braga particularly enjoyed taking up the baton. A talented musician, Braga had made a fortune in Paris, but his worrisome tendency to squander away his money prompted the countess to take personal control of his finances.

In fewer seasons than it takes to tell the story, Casa Venini became a hotbed of musical activity whose reputation resonated all the way to Milan. The correspondence exchanged among its many brilliant guests depicts a house transformed into a "salon for artists and amateurs," known for its marionette shows and "frequented by the most amusing and outlandish personalities in this world." In addition, the countess was also very pious, she had a small lane built across her grounds to offer religious processions an easier route than the main road.

Luisa Campioni Venini had many close friends, some of such high rank that only a throne could further elevate them in society. On a humbler level, she cultivated a long and cherished friendship with another regular guest, and perhaps the only one to endow the villa with a true literary legacy, albeit in indirect allusions. Antonio Fogazzaro* drew inspiration from the villa, its denizens, and their personal dramas for his novel *Piccolo Mondo Antico*, written in 1895 and still a treasured classic of Italian literature. In 1903, the Venini* heirs sold the villa to the Angerer-Comelli family, who in turn sold it in 1926 to Count Ottorino Mapelli, who left it to his children. Renamed Villa Mapelli, the estate was no longer widely mentioned except in travel guides—like *Paesaggi Lombardi* from 1934, a collection of travel reminiscences by Alex Visconti, who described it as "nestled in an evocative garden that tumbles down toward the lake." The designer and his children, friends, and associates refer to it as "the lake house," or more laconically "*la casa di Varenna*," adding "*sul lago*," on the lake. Those who have the pleasure of arriving at the house via the lake come ashore before reaching the Varenna waterfront, at a wooden dock reserved for dinghies, taxi-boats, and other small watercraft. Anything larger is advised to use the *traghetti* pier, further up on the port side.

A few steps along a suspended walkway, through an iron door that has to be unlocked, and we enter the estate. Its plants trained in espalier, as dictated by the relief and topography of the terrain, the garden is laid out in narrow terraces that offer a botanical profusion, a blend of Mediterranean and exotic species, evergreens, tall timber, and seasonal blossoms. A garden that bears no organic relation to the geometric symmetry of the house itself, which, seen from below, seems abruptly imposing. The path, necessarily winding as it connects one terrace to the next, is punctuated with places to sit, catch one's breath, contemplate the horizon, and smell the flowers. The shady spots with the nicest views have been equipped with gazebos, benches, and pavilions—constructions conceived purely for admiring the landscape, jewel-like in its beauty, glimpsed between two pines or from behind an exuberant floral thicket.

Seeking to enjoy his home outdoors as much as indoors, Sozzi has installed, with his characteristic elegance, informal alfresco sitting and dining areas paved with stone or wooden cubes. Embracing nature is an integral part of *savoir vivre*. Here and there, emerging from a rippling carpet or mossy green wave of vegetation, are peculiar perforated lighting devices, like antennae of vintage sci-fi aliens lurking in the greenery. Another curiosity to be discovered along the path: the four gray marble headstones in memory of Jack, Gin, Bulj, and Beautj, the late Countess Mapelli's beloved dogs.

With its stands of birch, cypress, and pine harboring a grotto, spanned by footbridges and a lovers' lane, the lush garden of Villa Mapelli was designed in the late eighteenth century by the architect **Giuseppe Jappelli*** according to Masonic principles. Just as he scoured the literature regarding the history of the lake, Varenna, and the house, surrounding himself with stacks of old books, albums, poetry collections, letters, and monographs, Romeo Sozzi researched the **garden*** in detail, compiling a precise index of its plants, variety by variety. He has the additional pleasure of observing the birds that nest in the trees, which he can identify by their chirping: swallows, tufted ducks, robins, sparrows, and his favorite, the blackbirds calling *kreek*, *kreek*, *kreek*.

[p. 34] ⟶

Born into an affluent Catholic family in Vicenza in 1842, Antonio Fogazzaro was one of very few writers from the newly unified Italy to attain both national and international prominence in his own lifetime. Trained as a lawyer, though he rarely practiced, Fogazzaro was married to the extremely wealthy Countess Margherita di Valmarana. Well-traveled, he achieved success with his first novel, *Malombra*, published in 1881. Driven by a religious sensibility at odds with the new Italian society, he was considered a "great poet of the future" after the triumph of his readings in Paris, and even served as a senator. He wrote many books, but *Piccolo Mondo Antico*, published in 1895 after the death of one of his three sons, remained the centerpiece of his oeuvre, as well as his greatest literary success. We know that many of his characters and settings were directly inspired by the Veninis and Villa Venini in Varenna, where Fogazzaro was a regular guest and a very dear friend of Countess Campioni Venini. The two exchanged a voluminous correspondence, which has been published in a collection. Five years later, Fogazzaro wrote a kind of sequel, *Piccolo Mondo Moderno*, steeped in religious fervor. His last two novels, *Il Santo* and *Leila*, fared less well: ill viewed by the Catholic Church, they were consigned to the Index of Prohibited Books.

Antonio Fogazzaro died during surgery in Vicenza in 1911. In 1941, *Piccolo Mondo Antico* was adapted for the screen by the writer-director Mario Soldati, with Massimo Serato, a popular young heartthrob of the day, and Alida Valli, who won the Volpi Cup at the Mostra di Venezia that same year, in the lead roles. Unofficially produced by Carlo Ponti, the film enjoyed immense popular success upon its release, largely due to its "anti-German temperament," in the words of the celebrated director Alberto Lattuada, who was then Soldati's assistant. In addition to scenes shot in the studios of Cinecittà, it was also filmed on location in Varenna and around the lake. Fogazzaro proved a propitious choice for Soldati once again in 1942 when he adapted *Malombra*, starring Isa Miranda, the grand diva of Italian cinema. Produced by Dino de Laurentiis, for whom it was a baptism by fire, *Malombra* was also a hit, again featuring sequences shot on Lake Como, this time in the sumptuous Villa Pliniana in Torno, once the property of the Belgiojoso princes, who played host to Napoléon, Liszt, Rossini, Puccini and, in a nice coincidence, Antonio Fogazzaro.

VENINI,
A HOUSE OF GLASS

It's one of the most prestigious glassworks in Murano. The name is respected worldwide, and makes collectors and curators prick up their ears. Formed in 1925 from the holdings of the defunct glassmaker Cappellin Venini & C., the *fornace* Vetri Soffiati Muranesi Venini & C. was soon known under the simpler name *Venini* in honor of one of its cofounders: Paolo Venini (1895–1959), a grandnephew of the former owners of Villa Venini, who gave up a career in law to pursue one of the oldest professions of the Venetian Lagoon. Working under the creative direction of Napoleone Martinuzzi, the house continued its nascent collaboration with the local sculptor Vittorio Zecchin, who had designed an iconic urn-shaped vase in 1921. Between 1932 and 47, Venini evolved radically under the firm artistic command of Carlo Scarpa, whose oeuvre became the foundation of the house's international reputation—especially with his famed molded-glass "handkerchief" vases, designed in 1940. After the war the house began inviting artists, architects, and designers to create projects in Murano, including Gio Ponti, Riccardo Licata, Tyra Lundgren, Tobia Scarpa, Tapio Wirkkala, and the brilliant Fulvio Bianconi. Before he died in 1959, bequeathing the business to his heirs, Paolo Venini also became a glass designer. His *Clessidra* hourglass, created in 1957, is now part of the brand's historical heritage. Today, virtually every artistically inclined architect and designer on the planet has teamed up with Venini, creating a vast body of work produced in very limited series or as one-of-a-kind creations. Alongside the big names in contemporary design, like Tadao Ando, Emmanuel Babled, Giorgio Vigna, Philippe Nigro, Rodolfo Dordoni, and Harri Koskinen, there is Laura Diaz de Santillana—the granddaughter of Paolo Venini.

It would be wrong to presume that this foray into glassmaking is something new in the history of the Veninis, one of the most prominent families of Varenna, dating back to 1388. Already in 1801, Bernardo Venini had opened a glassworks in Fiumelatte, taking advantage of the area's numerous silica deposits. Employing mainly Alsatian and German workers (because they were not obliged to abstain from meat on Fridays), the first Venini glass factory produced bottles that were sold in Milan, Bologna, Verona, and Venice. It closed in 1844 and moved to Trentino—and has no geographic or historical link to the Venetian glass design house founded by Paolo Venini.

For those who come to the lake house in Varenna by road there are no visible clues, other than the peaceful opulence of the entire area, to the beauty of the site. Paved with granite laid in fan shapes, the main street winds between a handful of old buildings, some completely covered with ivy. No sidewalk, no stoop: the entrance to the house looks like that of any house in the village: austere. On the other hand, the curved walls are a lustrous shade of ochre, and the scene is not without an element of ironic charm: across the road, a stone fountain spouts water from a tiny brass spigot fit for a dollhouse, over which one can read a surly warning dated 1907: "*Vietato lavare et lordare*" (No washing, no soiling). A dark green wooden double door, topped with a miter-shaped gray stone and adorned with two gleaming knockers, the house's entrance is staid, almost secret, as though making an effort not to intimidate the visitor. But just inside, the entrance becomes theatrical, an effect delivered by a heavy velvet curtain that opens onto a corridor leading straight to the light of the lake. The space is occupied by a table of trompe l'oeil proportions loaded with books, flowers, and trinkets, for which Sozzi has a special fondness. The people of Varenna are said, rightly, to be friendly and obliging, with a reputation for courtesy and elegant manners. Romeo Sozzi could not have chosen a better location. Welcome to his home, his house by the lake. And the surprise implied by the invitation? A jazz concert, on the water.

◆ GIUSEPPE JAPPELLI, ARCHITECT OF THE MASONIC GARDENS

A dyed-in-the-wool Venetian, the architect Giuseppe Jappelli (1783–1852) was one of Italy's most renowned garden designers of the early nineteenth century. His reputation blossomed after he completed the garden of Villa Sommi Picenardi in Cremona, and spread all the way to Britain, where he joined the Masonic order in 1806. Not long after, in 1816, he began work on the Veneto region's first Masonic garden at the Villa Citta-della-Vigodarzere (now Villa Valmarana), a romantic vision that included waterfalls, hills, and a lake. The creator of countless English-style gardens adorning the grand villas of the Veneto region, Jappelli also designed magnificent gardens in Padua (Treves, Pacchierotti, Giacomini, Romiati, for example), where he also built the famous Caffè Pedrocchi in 1842. Always tinged with a (perfectly legitimate) Masonic aura, the architect was invited by Prince Alessandro Torlonia to reconfigure the grounds of Villa Torlonia in Rome. In Varenna, his authorship is considerably less certain, and though Villa Venini's gardens are attributed to Jappelli, this should be taken with a grain of salt. Nonetheless, all of the elements of the Masonic garden are present: for example, the maternal cave, the overpasses, the birches at the water's edge, and the cypresses.

◆ THE VILLA MAPELLI GARDEN, SPECIES AND SPECIFICATIONS

No one does anything halfway here. Especially not Romeo Sozzi, who keeps a meticulous directory of all the botanical species planted in the garden of his house. They include evergreen trees such as acacia, camellia, *Laurus nobilis*, *Pinus pinaster*, and *Yucca speciosa*, evergreen shrubs like rhododendron and gaultheria, and deciduous varieties like *Prunus serrulata Kanzan*, *Betula pendula*, *Sambucus*, *Frangula*, hydrangea, and *filadelfi*. And, of course, the spectacular wisteria plant that engulfs the house's terrace and cascades down to the upper levels of the garden.

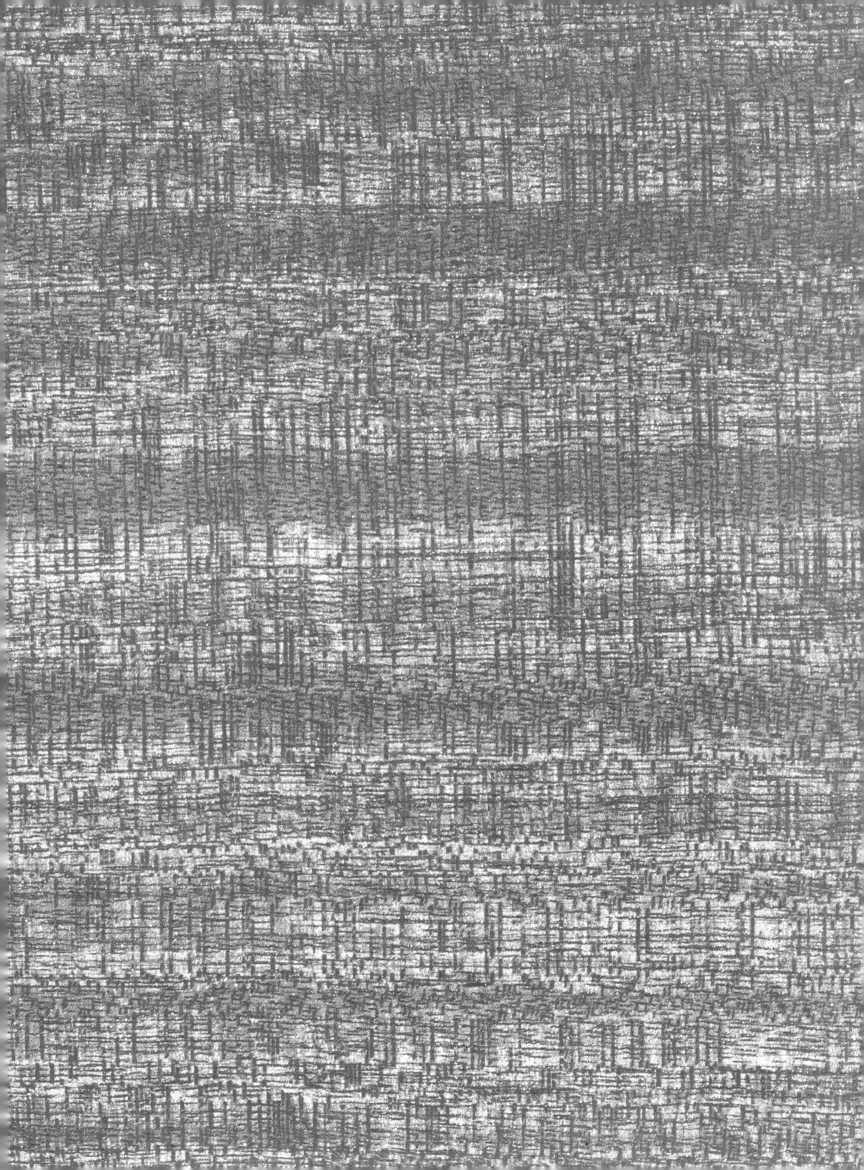

ROOM⁽ˢ⁾
FOR CHANGE

Romeo Sozzi's lakeside house in Varenna, historically known as Villa Mapelli, is what Italians commonly call *una dimora*. The word harbors several meanings under one roof: residence, retreat, family home, and, possibly, refuge, a place filled with memories offering or evoking seclusion. This house is all of those things, but in no sense an ivory tower, or a house merely for show. Even though he entertains many guests, this is where Sozzi lives. His children, now grownups with spouses, families, and homes of their own, also come and go. He has a full-time housekeeper who takes care of everything. The designer might slip out to meet friends for a lunch of *spaghetti aglio, olio e peperoncino*, come home, take off again, return two hours or two days later, get up at the first light of dawn to hike in the mountains, relax with a glass of white wine, decide to dine on the terrace, or stay indoors to read. With a feline independence, Sozzi never stays put.

He remodeled his house with painstaking care, assiduously avoiding the traps of historical or pseudo-historical reconstitution—he refuses to live in a museum. The man who once fantasized about a glass cube surrounded by nature has switched gears, taking advantage of this serendipitous opportunity to envision original solutions and revive traditional ones, transposing them into an innovative contemporary mode. Even better, by resurrecting a house that was falling into neglect, he has given it a new spirit while creating the illusion that everything was just like this a hundred years ago, only enhanced by his modern-day tastes. The mastermind of the place, Sozzi manages the house with both passion and patience, continually rotating the furniture and decorations as though they were props on a stage or movie set, striving for the best possible effects without leaving anything static. There is one overriding rule: to keep things moving depending on the arrivals—the new Promemoria furniture and accessories that are tested here, along with pieces discovered in antique stores in Milan, London, and Paris.

When Romeo Sozzi acquired it in 2001, Villa Mapelli looked in good shape. The exteriors, protected by the Italian Monuments and Fine Arts Department, had been preserved. Sozzi sent a nice letter to this venerable Italian institution—known

to be overly fussy in its strong protection of the country's incredible cultural heritage—and then did a trial run with three shades of yellow to find the right nuance to go with the gray doors, windows, terraces, and other ornaments, helping the facade recover its color and character. In contrast, the interiors were in a sorry state—not so much damaged as disfigured by a series of ill-conceived rearrangements and refurbishments. The house was broken up, empty, practically abandoned, and urgently needed renovation.

The work would last five years, preceded by eight months of sketching out floorplans, tearing down walls on paper, reconfiguring the rooms and spaces at the drawing board. Little by little, the discovery of hidden granite pillars, walled-over columns, plastered-over doors, forgotten stone staircases, and camouflaged painted ceilings made it necessary to modify the plan, taking it in a new direction, relaunching it like a pinball off a flipper. Sozzi took great pleasure in the project, enriching it with his own whims and taking it higher every step of the way, playing up and playing with the structure's idiosyncrasies, like its twenty different types of doors and twenty types of windows, from double-leaf French models to grilled basement vents.

Shortly after starting, well before anything was finished, he moved in, like a military commander on bivouac in the field. He had a bed, a chair, a lamp, and that was it. "I came here to understand what needed to be done," he says, "to study the daylight, the light of the lake, camping in every room. By moving around, I was able to perceive the broad outlines of the house's life force. The biggest problem was choosing the colors of the fabrics, because the light from the lake changes every three minutes!" Since he had chosen gray without deciding on the exact shade, Sozzi had the idea of making some twenty large panels lined with burlap in as many different tones of gray, and installing them in every room on every floor to determine the best nuance—a color that would be both neutral and personal. But the experiment failed: "In the time it took to go from one floor to another, the color of the lake would change, and the color of the panel would gain or lose some of its impact and intensity." Out with burlap, in with linen… but still no conclusive results. Sozzi then tried stretching the panels with velvet. That did it. The surface, the material, the shades—pigeon gray downstairs, powdery pink upstairs—suddenly echoed the lake, absorbing, replicating, and beautifying its light. "Then, as soon as

I could," he recounts, "I brought in other pieces of furniture, all different kinds of seats in order to experience the house."

Finally the long-awaited day came: time to move in. Time to turn the heavy iron key in the lock of the main entrance. Not much furniture inside. And no heat—the roof was still being repaired. Out of a need to acclimate himself and assimilate his new surroundings, the designer spent hours on the terrace contemplating the lake, sipping liters of green tea, and later, as the sun began to dip toward the horizon, his beloved dry martinis. ("I plugged in a fridge and an icemaker long before the house was even finished.") Standing on his terrace, a dandy down to the shape of the glass in his hand, Sozzi doesn't see his station in life as vindication. Born and raised on Lake Como, in the ancient village of Valmadrera, he laughingly recalls the shore in the summer, family vacation destinations then seen and savored as fabulous, and later teenage adventures on a motorboat with just enough money to buy gas for the crossing, leaving nearly nothing for a soda. The fact remains that by adapting this house, which has been part of so many lives, to his personal lifestyle, Sozzi has, in his own way, restored its soul.

But back to the materials. What about the floors? Opaque black stone? "Too modern, too hard." Sozzi chose old-fashioned parquet, but in antique oak. There is no attempt to imitate any period or style. But even after this alchemy became a reality, no decision was final. Sozzi never tires of altering, modifying, replacing, and fine-tuning. In his home and in his head, the slightest change—a cabinet knob, a table, a chair, a color, a variety of wood, of leather— turns the entire room around like a carousel, which then undergo changes of their own. This interaction is one of the keystones of Sozzi's success, an indicator of his versatility, and the unifying thread of his inexhaustible creativity. His early days in Varenna went by in a flash, in a mixture of enthusiasm and anxiety. Had he done something rash? Yes, but it wouldn't be the first time—or the last.

"I wanted materials that express masculinity," he explains, *"knowing that femininity would come through in the choice of fabrics and décor."*

A visit to the Varenna house is not like a visit to the showroom on Via Bagutta in Milan. The lake house doesn't have visitors, it has guests; guests who are invited to revel in an inspiring *dolce far niente*, in which even the smallest detail creates a

superlative break from routine. Rarely has a private home had so much to teach even the most demanding hoteliers. If Romeo Sozzi were not a creator of superb furniture, he could easily be a consultant to the world's top hotels. A challenge for the future, perhaps?

Comprising a central structure built in a neoclassical style in the mid-seventeenth century, and expanded in the eighteenth with the addition of two symmetrical wings by an unidentified architect, Villa Mapelli does not boast the palatial dimensions of the other famous villas on Lake Como. It's a family home, peaceful and comfortable, not a showcase of pomp and vanity. In that sense it is more closely related to the regal villas along the Elba in Hamburg, much admired by the architectural disciples of Karl Friedrich Schinkel. Romeo Sozzi's lakeside house emanates an unassuming aura in which true luxury is conveyed through the culture and erudition of its owner, a man of wide-ranging curiosity, a lover of music and books, a collector of frog figurines and Jaguars, a bon vivant and so much more.

With its adjoining sitting rooms, dining room, lounges, kitchen, study, and private chambers, the ground floor is the *piano nobile* (the main part of the house), with the upper level reserved for the guest rooms, which show the same degree of decorative care. Sozzi, naturally, lives mostly on the "noble" floor, at the same level as the street but high above the lake on the other side, commanding a panoramic view. The master of every aspect of his domain, he has invented and implemented a cagey system using solid volumes whose openings become tableaux framed by structural components, exactly as a car designer conceives the interior of a convertible. Several of the doors, including the one to the kitchen, have been moved to offer direct views of the lake; the pleasures of the palate and a feast for the eyes.

Every corner of every room exudes a nonchalant chic calibrated down to the millimeter and the Pantone number. In these forest-like interiors, the smallest object, however commonplace, tells its own little story, weaves its own plot. "The extraordinary is hidden in the details," Sozzi likes to say. Here, hidden under the woodwork and velvet panels, are the technical requisites of modern-day comfort. Somewhere behind the scenes, there has to be a system for heating and cooling the house, whose entryway leads straight toward the light of a broad window framing a charmingly gnarled bonsai. In the background loom the outlines of the mountains overlooking Menaggio, on the other side of the lake. Punctuated by four lamps

standing on the antique oak-framed inlaid panel parquet, their glow muted by silk shades, the space is nearly filled by a long narrow table covered in damask velvet. A table that creates a trompe l'oeil effect due to its trapezoidal shape: $A=(B+b)\times H/2$. In layman's terms: a play on perspective. Placed, more so than arranged, upon it is an array of objects bearing eloquent witness to Romeo Sozzi's interests and fancies: colored glass fish, jellyfish paperweights, and a few of his cherished frog figurines. And, speaking of the designer's passions, books, of course. One is entitled *Vivere con il Legno* ("Living with Wood"), and another is a monograph devoted to Eyre de Lanux, an American designer who was active in Paris in the Roaring Twenties, an era that the master of the house finds inspiring. Of noble birth, she became a pre-modern creative force foreshadowing Eileen Gray—the kind of personality that Sozzi prizes, like the characters in the novels that he devours one after the other.

And now to the sitting room: the formula may be old school, but it still works. For Italian film buffs, the room conjures up images of *Venga a Prendere il Caffè da Noi (Come Have Coffee With Us)*, a cruel black comedy from the 1970s starring Ugo Tognazzi and Milena Vukotic. Shot in Luino, on the shore of Lake Maggiore, it tells the tale of a large old house where three spinster sisters spend a great deal of time in the parlor flirting with an alpha male, who ends up out of action in a wheelchair. The scenario is much different at Villa Mapelli, except for the coffee and the bowls brimming with candies that he nibbles distractedly while deciding where to sit and continue the conversation under the decorated ceilings of the Four Seasons room. And it's quite a decision, because the designer has filled the velvet- and silk-swathed alcoves with a panoply of sofas, divans, love seats, ottomans, armchairs, and *bergères*, mixing periods and styles from classic French to vintage Swedish to plush contemporary Promemoria. So many objects and details catch the eye that it's almost possible to overlook the restored frescoes on the ceiling, whose seasonal themes set the tone. Lovely, delicate, and delectably allegorical, the scenes adorning this decorative firmament can be traced back to the eighteenth century, but not so easily to the artist who painted them. Though we can only guess, they are presumed to be the work of an artist known as "Lapriani." There is no documentation to prove it, but Sozzi mentions that this mysterious Lapriani painted the ceilings of a great many villas on the lake—so why not here? A question that sparks—in the celestial aura of this wonderfully chromatic opus—a diverting and digressing conversation

about all the artists, famous and obscure, who came to write, paint, or compose here or nearby. The host himself has conceived a composition of materials and colors that transmutes the door frames, piers, moldings, and graceful scrolls into a sprinkling of colorful and monochromatic accents—the art of modernizing, subtly but boldly, ultra-classical elements paired with radical treatments or lighthearted fantasies. Here, the Murano glass chandeliers bring to mind bouquets of crystalline orchids, shedding light on a man of such taste that he can blithely blend art deco with ethnic art, black and white with the most delicate color, and frogs of every description with Murano vases from the forties and fifties by Barovier or Venini.

Other spaces, other rooms—sprawling in the vastness of the house's north wing: A black lacquered grand piano; outsized sofas, including a **Gio Ponti** vintage model; an enormous bookcase lining a long wall; other monumental pieces... This is a space on a different scale, nearly opulent—even though the goal was simply to make use of the space and volumes centering around a gigantic granite pillar. We circle it as though playing hide-and-seek, furtively stroking its surface in the hope of absorbing some of the stone's vital energy. The presence of the bookcase reconfirms the importance of its contents—for Sozzi, **books** are an essential component of any living space. And it's not just for show: all of the books that are stored, stacked, and categorized here have been read and reflected on, more than just once, including intriguing volumes like the *Almanacco della Famiglia Meneghina*, 1933 to 1941, a curiosity for bibliophiles. The art books lying on the huge coffee table reflect our host's current interests, including Leonardo da Vinci, Riva motorboats, and the photo album *Afghan Gold* by Luke Powell.

Between these two sitting rooms, interpolated in the way that people used to set up tables to have lunch, tea, or dinner in the same parlor where they entertained company, or themselves with games and solitaire, the dining room adapts to any and all uses. Furnished with a Brazil nut wood table, velvet-upholstered *Isotta chairs*, and two traditional Italian armchairs, its strategic advantage is its immediate proximity to the kitchen, in which Sozzi did not content himself with half-baked décor. Quite the contrary: the walls are a coral-tinged shade of orange, the ventilation hood encrusted with beveled mirrors like those once used to primp up vanity tables and boudoir furniture, the brushed steel and the battery of leading-edge

[p. 64] ⟶

◆ GIO PONTI, THE LUMINARY
OF TWENTIETH-CENTURY ITALIAN DESIGN

He was the protean inventor of twentieth-century Italian design. Born and raised in Milan, son of the director of the powerful Edison company, the protean Gio Ponti (1891–1979) did everything, designed everything, built everything. Lamps, buildings, fabrics, churches, bathroom sinks, hotels, furniture, magazines, ocean liners, trains—even costumes for La Scala. Not a single sector or discipline escaped his influence. Most often teaming up with illustrious collaborators, from Emilio Lancia to Pier Luigi Nervi and Piero Fornasetti, Ponti was the most prolific progettista (no one said "designer" back then) in the history of Italian architecture and industrial design, as well as the decorative arts, for which he became an eminent ambassador, exporting his vision around the world: to São Paulo with the Faculty of Nuclear Physics, Caracas with Villa Planchart, Tehran with Villa Nemazee, Colorado with the Denver Art Museum. In his home city, he left an exemplary architectural heritage ranging from the Palazzo Rasini, adjoining the Bastions of Porta Venezia, to the Pirelli Tower, Milan's tallest skyscraper for many years, but now surpassed by the new towers of Porta Nuova. Ponti also built the reputation of the Triennale (formerly the Monza Biennial), the interior design fair held every three years within the august walls of the Palazzo dell'Arte built by Giovanni Muzio. After World War II, Ponti worked extensively for the Rinascente department store chain. It was his idea to initiate the national prize that would become the Compasso d'Oro. Now considered the "Oscar of design," it was first conceived to highlight the formal and contemporary quality of mass-produced objects (still before people spoke of "design"). Ponti's talent and ability made him much in demand as an artistic director for brands like the centuries-old porcelain maker Richard Ginori, and he worked for many houses, usually over long periods with the occasional hiatus for other creative projects. In 1928 he founded Domus, a journal created to promote the basic precepts of Modernism, and which carried a lot of weight in both the kiosks and the public memory. In addition to his work for the French silversmiths Christofle and Puiforcat, the German Walter Krupp and the Fontana Arte glassworks, Ponti also created the fittings for the ultra-modern Settebello express train, plus, in 1951, the interiors of the twin passenger ships Andrea Doria and Giulio Cesare, veritable oceangoing embassies for Italy's fine and decorative arts. Ponti's furniture designs are still produced by Cassina, but his heritage goes beyond that, serenely exerting its presence at estate sales and auctions due to the innumerable interiors that he created for private houses and apartments, all with made-to-measure pieces that remain one-of-a-kind. Today, Romeo Sozzi admires and studies the brilliant legacy of Gio Ponti, the ingenious engineer who could do anything—including work with wood as skillfully as a master cabinetmaker.

A MAN AND HIS BOOKS: ROMEO SOZZI'S
READING LIST FOR JUNE 2015

This list was compiled based on the books left within easy reach in Romeo Sozzi's bedroom at his house in Varenna, where his shelves overflow with travel guides, essays, monographs, art books, novels, biographies, albums, and dictionaries. Listed in no systematic or preferential order, they reflect the designer's tastes, interests, and passions, as well as his insatiable curiosity for books of all kinds.

- *Note di Cucina di Leonardo da Vinci (Leonardo's Kitchen Note Books)* by Shelagh and Jonathan Routh.
- A monograph on Max Ingrand, known for his work as artistic director of Fontana Arte.
- *Se Non Ora, Quando? (If Not Now, When?)* by Primo Levi.
- A James Ensor monograph.
- *Il Novecento Antico.*
- *Il Calzolaio Prodigioso*, a luxury edition biography of shoemaker to the stars Salvatore Ferragamo.
- *Women Are Heroes*, an album on the work of the guerilla street artist JR.
- *La Conquista del Tempo*, a reference book on the history of timepieces.
- *Il Caso Rembrandt (The Rembrandt Affair)*, a thriller by Daniel Silva.
- *La Dolce Vita* as seen by the American photographer Slim Aarons.
- *La Villa Kerylos*, French edition with a preface by Karl Lagerfeld.
- *Carl Auböck: The Workshop*, by Clemens Kois and Brian Janusiak, a monumental inventory of the work of this Austrian modernist artisan.

- *Le Dictionnaire des Arts de l'Islam* (French dictionary of Islamic art).
- *Axel Vervoordt, Esprit Wabi*—otherwise known as Zen and the Art of European Decoration.
- *L'Avventura del Design*, devoted to the Bologna-based designer and manufacturer Dino Gavina, who produced the furniture of Sebastian Matta, among others.
- *Mobilier National 1964–2004*, a catalog of the purchases, orders, and reserves of the French national furniture depository, which traces its history back to the kings' royal storehouses.
- *Caratteri e tipografia del XX Secolo (Twentieth Century Typography)*, indicative of Sozzi's fascination with printing and publishing.
- A rare French monograph devoted to *Dominique*, the design house founded in 1922 by the decorators André Domin and Marcel Genevrière, which supplied the furniture for the Normandie ocean liner.
- *Italiani*, an album by Gianni Berengo Gardin, the other great Italian photojournalist whose visual sensibility Sozzi admires.

appliances make it the perfect place to enjoy an apéritif or an ice cream at the counter, chatting and snacking on fruit or peanuts. Not to mention the cupboards tucked away under the low ceilings, marked by patterns of expressionist colors that suggest and emphasize the labyrinthine aspect of the space. Unlike so many Italian houses, in which the kitchen remains a protected enclave of docile domesticity, at Villa Mapelli it's a vibrant hub of activity, rooted in the spirit of the place—a convivial setting conducive to spontaneous sharing and interaction, and in that sense a reflection of its owner's personality.

To the left on the way out, the elegant two-piece sideboard-bar, a Ponti-esque Italian model from the 1950s, duly restored, stores the antique glassware that Sozzi enjoys collecting. When turning his attention to the preparation of his favorite drink, the dry martini, he might well ask a guest to fetch the appropriate glasses from the sideboard. It's all part of the atmosphere of trust—unless it's just the alluring mystery of old closets and cabinets, and the unspoken hope of discovering hidden secrets.

The wisteria-covered terrace overlooking the lake is the house's extra room. The outdoor extension is essential to the Italian-style art of living and Sozzi has turned the terrace into a theater loge from which to view the stunning scenery, without marring the outdoor area's charming structural simplicity. It is the center of daily life during the warm months, starting at breakfast time, which for the designer means 6:30 a.m. But it is also so in winter, when the weather is mild or when the lake is shrouded in early morning fog, an otherworldly vision enlivened by the lights of the *traghetti*, which give the lake the look of a misty merry-go-round. It is indeed about the view—but more than that, because the terrace, open to nature, acts as a barometer, a calendar marking the days between light and silence, it is the inspiration for Sozzi's 2015 Promemoria furniture collection entitled *Lake Tales*. In the center of the terrace, the designer has placed a yellow marble table, an incredible oval-shaped amber-gold surface that seems to have swallowed a liquid sun. The color of the espresso served in black and ochre Anduze ceramic cups generates palpable vibrations. The vibrations are actually coming from Sozzi's cell phone. On the water below, a rubber dinghy leads a convoy of little boats from a sailing school. "Is that you down on the lake? No?" It is both a terrace and a crow's nest.

Reserving the upper floor for the comfort and privacy of his overnight guests, Romeo Sozzi made one of the handsomest ground-floor rooms of the south wing

his personal domain. His office and reading room, lit by windows that open onto views of both garden and lake, this intimate space is nestled under a bayed and coffered ceiling studded with eighteenth-century sculpted, patinated wooden cabochons, where he can rest his gaze between pages while lying on a magnificent solid rosewood bed of his own design. Like the other rooms of the house, settings for faster-paced activities, Sozzi's bedroom is truly a compendium of his interests and aesthetic impulses, overlaid with a comforting, tranquil, stimulating profusion of books, objects, and accessories, tokens of an intellect on perpetual alert. His nightstands bear the proof, holding stacks of books, including such literary oddities as Jan Potocki's *The Manuscript Found in Saragossa* and Dario Vergassola's *La Ballata delle Acciughe (Ballad of the Anchovy)*.

From the ebony *Bonaventura* commode to the mahogany *Amleto* bookcase-desk, both Promemoria atelier pieces, to the antique reading table and the old flat Louis Vuitton Monogram trunk that Sozzi found in Paris (a souvenir of the travels of an unknown dandy now forgotten but for his painted initials), every piece of furniture is laden with books. As for the recently added wall shelves, they are already overflowing with books, plus countless objects for which the meaning and purpose can only be imagined. Only the imposing, red Verona marble fireplace escapes the inundation of books, along with two eighteenth-century, velvet-lined Genoa chairs and the capacious rosewood-and-leather armchair by **Ico Parisi*** from the end of the 1950s. Completing the tableau, meticulously framed black-and-white photos commemorate the close friendship between Sozzi, a photography lover, and the great photographer Mario De Biasi.

Lastly, the master bathroom commands an even greater degree of privacy. Suffice it to say that Sozzi's, concealed behind a secret door in his reading room, is in black Marquina marble, chosen in reference to the marble that was once quarried in Fiumelatte and Varenna, with a teak bathtub and a bronze towel holder. The room includes other fixtures that need no detailed description.

Among its many curiosities, the lake villa houses an elevator with a cabin as luxurious as a yacht. One might expect it to lead down to the shore or the pier, but no—we're not in Amalfi or Ravello. It only links the three levels of the house, from the bowels of the cellar to the guest suites on the top floor. It also makes it possible to go for a dip in the black granite covered pool with underwater lighting, or for a

[p. 70] ⟶

ICO PARISI

Born Domenico Parisi in Palermo in 1916, raised in Lombardy from the age of four, the architect Ico Parisi is the most original and least known of the great Italian *progettisti* of the twentieth century—and the most eccentric, zealously defying all labels and categories. Discreetly esteemed in his home country but still known only to connoisseurs outside of Italy, Parisi, "Il Pà" to his friends, was a close associate of prominent abstract painters like Radice, Badiali, and Rho. He was also a student and, although still young, collaborator with the Rationalist architect Giuseppe Terragni, for whom he took the official photographs of Casa del Fascio in Como and Villa Bianca in Seveso. His involvement in the Cinegulf in Como led him to produce a documentary entitled *Como+Como+Como*. After the war, in which he fought on the Russian Front, Parisi opened his own agency-workshop-showroom in Como: La Ruota, dedicated to interior and furniture design, and an outlet for his avant-garde creations. In demand as far away as Paris, where he exhibited at the 34th SAD (*Salon des Artistes Décorateurs*) decorative arts fair, Parisi created a string of pieces for Cassina including the iconic Uovo chair, experimented with ceramics, glass, and jewelry, and specialized in designing sets for exhibitions like the *Mostra del Giornalismo in Milan.*

His artistic sensibility brought him into contact again with Radice, as well as Lucio Fontana and Bruno Munari, with whom he envisioned a series of projects in the early 1950s conceived as a synthesis of art and architecture. Their effort resulted in buildings like Casa Carcano in Maslianico, the Camera di Commercio, Industria e Agricoltura in Sondrio, and the Padiglione Soggiorno for the 10th Milan Triennale in 1954, a pa-

vilion that later became the Parco Sempione Library. The next few years brought collaborations with singular artists like Enrico Baj and the Gruppo T collective. Parisi's work with the respected French art critic Pierre Restany, a champion of New Realism, came to fruition in two projects, *Ipotesi per una Casa Esistenziale* (1972) and *Operazione Arcevia Comunità Esistenziale* (1974), with contributions by the artists Duane Hanson, César, and Alberto Burri, as well as the author and screenwriter Tonino Guerra and the filmmaker Michelangelo Antonioni. The artistic quality of *Operazione Arcevia* earned it a place at the 1976 Venice Biennale, where Parisi was featured again two years later with *Libertà è Uscire Dalla Scatola (freedom is breaking out of the box)*, an artistic-architectural work included in the *Utopies* series. It and the other utopias were then exhibited in Rome, Brussels, Ferrara, and Kassel, at the *Documenta* exhibition.

In the 1980s the retrospectives began, the first taking place at PAC (Padiglione d'Arte Contemporanea) in Milan in 1986 under the sweeping title of *Ico Parisi: l'Officina del Possibile.* Later came *Ico Parisi: & Architecture* in 1990, followed by *Ico Parisi: & Disegni* in 1994 at the Galleria Civica in Modena. Looking back on this visionary's life and career, one can easily understand Romeo Sozzi's admiration for Parisi, who chose to live and work in Como, where he died in 1996, and where, for a performance, he once transformed Piazza Cavour into a maze of garbage to make people think about the effects of consumer society. A versatile creator equally at ease designing office furniture or sumptuous rosewood and leather armchairs, Ico Parisi is remembered as a genius who remained aloof from all cliques.

workout in the gym under the massive red vaults without having to parade through the rest of the house scantily clad. Of course, there are also the stairs, which offer their own form of aerobic exercise: running down to the garden or the lake and climbing back up. The staircase that connects the ground floor with the upper level is more evocative, highlighted by the décor but retaining a certain monastic austerity, a reminder that in the eighteenth century, and even later, people didn't make such a fuss about moving from floor to floor. Carpeted in gray velvet, lit by Viennese crystal and deepened by an oversized inclined mirror (the Promemoria *Michelle* model), this stairway leads to the guest floor. At the top are corridors to the right and left, each one leading to two suites with herringbone parquet floors, decorated more concisely but without budging a millimeter from the criteria of luxury and excellence that have forged Sozzi's reputation. A *Theo* desk, *Bilou Bilou* chairs, and a constellation of silk and velvet cushions. Details worthy of a five-star hotel, including the carefully plotted placement of the linen-bedecked beds: facing the windows, they offer an image of the *traghetti* gliding across the lake that couldn't be more perfectly framed with a classic Leica. No one would dream of closing the gray wooden shutters at bedtime.

Even in the dark of night, the lake murmurs and whispers. Secreted behind the stately wooden headboards, the bathrooms are scented with Acqua di Parma cologne and stocked with everything that a guest might need—or have forgotten. This floor also has its curio: a cabinet neither antique nor Caligarian. A gigantic cabinet for a giant in velvet kneepants, a cabinet named *George*. This *George* stores Romeo Sozzi's summer clothes in the winter, and his winter clothes in the summer. Behind the glass doors, it's lavishly adorned with gold fabric. Sozzi doesn't mind mocking his own vanity, making *George* both a wardrobe and a display case. A double cabinet lined with Japanese-patterned paper where his vanities are unabashedly arrayed. And where we'd love to play hide and seek like children, just to see what we could find.

FROM MILAN TO...

Milan is the capital of Lombardy, and it's the economic and financial capital of Italy, the home of the Italian stock market. But Milan is also the world capital of design. All of the major design firms and furniture brands are established here

with their showrooms and galleries, and most of them have factories in the region. While Brianza, north of Milan, remains the historical cradle of the Italian home furnishings industry, the areas around Como and Lecco are also part of this hub. Romeo Sozzi's Promemoria atelier has its headquarters in Valmadrera, just across the lake from Lecco, and showrooms in the world's major capitals, from London to Moscow, from Paris to New York, and, of course, Milan. To meet the obligations of his professional life, as well as his social life (including evenings at **La Scala,** where he shares a box with a small group of friends), Sozzi has an apartment in the city. It is nothing comparable to the nearby Villa Necchi Campiglio, a residence built in the 1930s by the architect Piero Portaluppi for the Necchi sisters, heiresses of their family's sewing machine fortune, who were tired of making the eighteen mile trip home to Pavia after a night in their box at La Scala. Their monumental villa, which was donated to the Fondo per l'Ambiente Italiano in 2001, houses the extraordinary Claudia Gian Ferrari collection of early twentieth-century art. Located on Via Mozart, it is a stone's throw from the famous Villa Invernizzi, where pink flamingos roam the grounds.

In the heart of Milan, surrounded by some of the city's most eclectic architecture, from paroxysmal "Liberty" art nouveau to Neo-Gothic, the designer leads exactly the same kind of life as in Varenna: going out, coming home, taking off again, entertaining, playing host to friends and to friends of friends, sending out invitations, presiding at dinners. Sometimes he opens his doors to small groups of curious-minded travelers on a tour of the world's great opera houses. They always leave enchanted and charmed by his hospitality and courteous attentions.

The décor of the apartment derives from the same principles and ideas as all of Sozzi's living spaces: hospitality, conviviality, revelry, and joie de vivre, combined with extreme refinement. The dining room, the sitting rooms which Cecil Beaton would have loved to photograph, and the library awash in books, are of course all furnished with chairs and other creations by Romeo Sozzi. These are pieces that define the image of Promemoria. And, as in Sozzi's other spaces, the furniture, lamps, and decorative objects are in perpetual motion, modifying the décor to the point of completely rearranging any given room. The acquisition of an antique or the arrival of a vintage piece restored in the Valmadrera workshops can trigger an upheaval, with the high probability of a textile transplant for the sofas and a chromatic about-face for the walls and drapes, or vice versa. And another object lesson

[p. 81] ⟶

◆ LA SCALA

It's the world's most famous shrine to the operatic arts, described by Stendhal as the grandest, most magnificent, and most imposing of all theaters. Built on the smoking ruins of the Teatro Ducale, which burned down in 1776, the Teatro alla Scala was commissioned by Maria Theresa of Austria, built by the architect Giuseppe Piermarini, and inaugurated in 1778 by Archduke Ferdinand with a performance of Salieri's *Europa Riconosciuta*. Accommodating 3,000 spectators, La Scala was also a hotbed of social life—especially in its well-known loges (box seats), which were the permanent property, passed on by inheritance, of the ninety most prominent Milanese families (including the Viscontis, in loge number four). The owners ate meals and gambled in their loges, glancing up once in a while to see what was happening on stage. Intense competition from Teatro San Carlo in Naples, combined with the impetus of certain loge owners with experience as producers and patrons (the Viscontis at the top of the list), raised La Scala to its pinnacle in the early nineteenth century, when it brought in Rossini, Bellini, and La Malibran, for instance, and later Giuseppe Verdi, who ensured the house's place in history when he virtually became its composer in residence starting in 1839.

The other great La Scala legend was Arturo Toscanini, who introduced revolutionary changes as music director, in particular eliminating the heredi-

tary ownership of the loges—a move so radical that the Milanese would have been less shocked if he had simply cut off a few heads.

Modernized, venerated, La Scala became the world's premier opera house—the Met in New York would hire no one who had not triumphed in Milan. Those who had included La Tebaldi, Mario del Monaco, Mirella Freni, Placido Domingo, Barbara Hendricks, and above all Maria Callas, who attained glory in 1955 in a production of *La Traviata* directed by Luchino Visconti. Renovated and expanded by the Swiss architect Mario Botta in 2004, La Scala entered the twenty-first century under the influential administrators and artistic directors Stéphane Lissner from France, followed by the Austrian Alexander Pereira, who updated the programming and imposed many changes on stage and in the hall, all the while adhering to a core set of principles that no one would ever dream of abandoning.

The season officially begins every year on December 7, the Feast of Sant'Ambrogio, patron saint of the city of Milan. The red carpet, A-list guests, flowing gowns, tuxedos, hordes of paparazzi—the opening is not only cultural, but also a political, social, and media event. Today, with ticket prices within reach for students and young music lovers, La Scala is less exclusive than before. But still, on opera night, everyone gives it their all in the wardrobe department.

in the designer's uncanny knack for smoothing over the seams, creating the illusion that the room has always looked like that. Wherever he is, wherever he lives, Sozzi wields a unique talent for creating peaceful havens. Some might see him as a decorative Zen master, but those who know the designer well are perfectly aware that under this apparent calm lies a constant, indefatigable effort. As for the furniture, versatile by nature, it moves around like so many Monopoly tokens.

Via dei Giardini is a sinuous leafy avenue off Via Manzoni, and is one of the most sought-after addresses in central Milan. Here Sozzi has found the ideal apartment that would fulfill his plan of converting it into a kitchen—the Angelina kitchen, named after his mother. And to have fun, to make *cucina* rhyme with *gioia*, playing different culinary accents like a pianist with a cutting board instead of a keyboard. Besides the kitchen itself, a masterpiece of decoration in which even the smallest hinge in the drawers for storing the pots and pans (copper, of course) is made of bronze, and even the shelves are lined with topstitched leather, the apartment houses a dining room, an all-glass wine cellar, sitting rooms, the bar cabinet *Bacco*, and an alabaster bathroom—all updated whenever Promemoria releases a new collection.

At ease everywhere around the globe, Romeo Sozzi has a special fondness for Paris, where he once kept an apartment on a curious L-shaped street in the heart of the Plaine Monceau area, between Wagram and Malesherbes. In the late nineteenth and early twentieth centuries, this was the favored district of the Parisian *haute bourgeoisie*, who built townhouses here in the Haussmann style that was then the pinnacle of good taste. This is the neighborhood where Françoise Sagan lived with her family when she published *Bonjour Tristesse* in 1954.

This is where Léo Malet set the plot of his 1959 novel *L'Envahissant Cadavre de la Plaine Monceau*, the fifteenth and final installment of his "New Mysteries of Paris" series recounting the adventures of the private detective Nestor Burma. This is where the French New Wave director Éric Rohmer filmed *La Boulangère de Monceau (The Bakery Girl of Monceau)*, the first of his *Six Moral Tales*, in 1962. Today the area has been neglected (or perhaps spared) by popular fads and trends—a plus for Sozzi, who still speaks with affection of its small shops and cafés.

BEHIND THE SCENES: MECHANICAL INSPIRATIONS

Whatever its function, wherever its location, each of Romeo Sozzi's homes deserves to be examined from every angle, like opening a music box to see the machinery at work. Under the floors, behind the walls, at the back of the cabinets, in the drawers of a sideboard, in the folding of a portable table, the designer devises impressively sophisticated mechanisms. From the doorjambs to the hinges, from the light switches to the wall plugs, from the intake vents to the blowers, he's a virtual Captain Nemo of design. While Jules Verne imagined an extravagant, elaborate future, Sozzi keeps pace with progress but takes care not to let it intrude on the décor. As a result, the technical elements are out of sight. And those that can't be invisible are inevitably elegant, even if it means casting them in bronze, each element bearing Sozzi's signature.

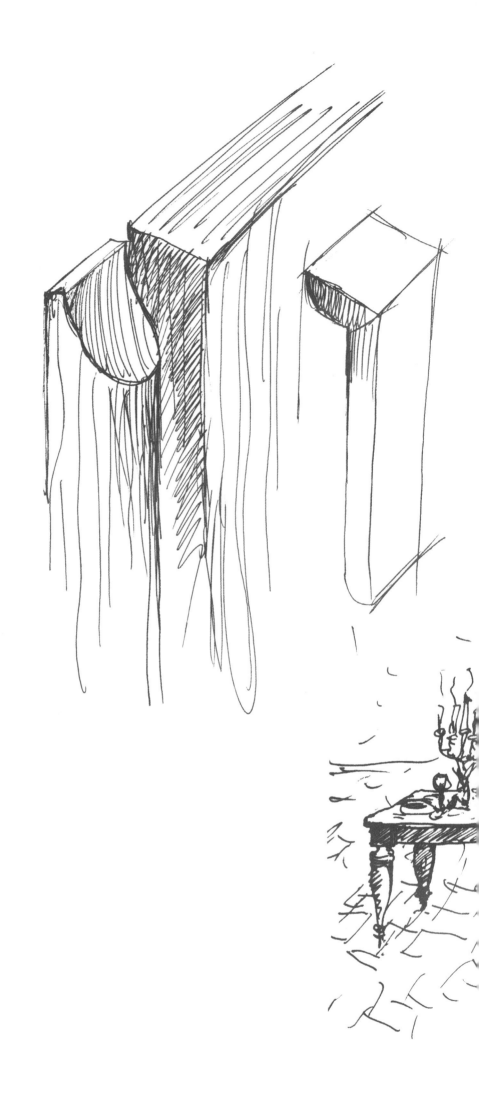

INTERTWINING
INTERESTS AND PASSIONS

Founder of the contemporary cabinetmaking company Promemoria, designer of superlatively beautiful furniture appreciated by connoisseurs around the world, and inventor of an art of living that merges simplicity with sophistication, Romeo Sozzi has always treated his own houses and apartments as laboratories for consecrating his creations—which in turn consecrate the rooms that they occupy. His lakeside house in Varenna and apartment in Milan are no exceptions to this rule, which also sets the exclusive standard for his Angelina showroom on Via dei Giardini in Milan, the reception area of his atelier in Valmadrera, and even his own office, a cluttered studio that serves as the inner sanctum and prime arena of his creativity. This is where, shielded from the commotion of the workshops, Sozzi reads, researches, reflects, reviews, draws, writes, rests, leaves, returns, stores his purchases and acquisitions, stacks up books, arranges furniture, furnishings, and paintings, or piles them up pending a decision on where they can go, where they can be of (re)use. While the Varennese house and the Milanese apartment, between personal moments and visits to the bedroom or library, subtly reveal multiple cultural indicators and insights as to their owner's character, his office in Valmadrera, with its expanse, its profusion, its multifunctionalism, and eclecticism, sheds the most light on the real Romeo Sozzi. Located on the building's second floor, the office is by no means a secret place, but one does not just walk in uninvited. Once inside there is the risk of getting lost, because the space is a maze, intuitively laid out, maintained, and reinforced by the office's occupant. It seems haphazard at first glance, but Sozzi knows instantly where everything is. Of course, sometimes—in fact often—in the late afternoon, when the overhead lamps on the pink-painted ceiling no longer emit enough light, he has to strap on a headlamp and clamber up the columns of books, rising from the floor like so many stalagmites, to fetch a particular tome from the top of a cave-like bookcase.

Whenever Sozzi travels, the trip begins and ends in this immense, carefully disordered room, in which each specific area, from the bar to the wardrobe to the cabinets for the collections, functions as a bastion made impregnable by congestion—and in

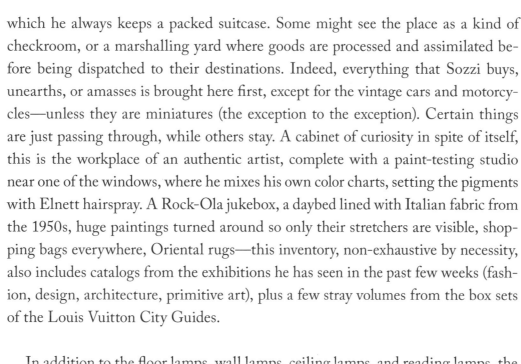

which he always keeps a packed suitcase. Some might see the place as a kind of checkroom, or a marshalling yard where goods are processed and assimilated before being dispatched to their destinations. Indeed, everything that Sozzi buys, unearths, or amasses is brought here first, except for the vintage cars and motorcycles—unless they are miniatures (the exception to the exception). Certain things are just passing through, while others stay. A cabinet of curiosity in spite of itself, this is the workplace of an authentic artist, complete with a paint-testing studio near one of the windows, where he mixes his own color charts, setting the pigments with Elnett hairspray. A Rock-Ola jukebox, a daybed lined with Italian fabric from the 1950s, huge paintings turned around so only their stretchers are visible, shopping bags everywhere, Oriental rugs—this inventory, non-exhaustive by necessity, also includes catalogs from the exhibitions he has seen in the past few weeks (fashion, design, architecture, primitive art), plus a few stray volumes from the box sets of the Louis Vuitton City Guides.

In addition to the floor lamps, wall lamps, ceiling lamps, and reading lamps, the furnishings consist of chairs, like the plump black leather *Elda* armchair by Joe Colombo, all buried under bulging folders, portfolios, document bags, and briefcases. Then there are the tables, low and high, round and square, all engulfed with magazines and catalogs. But the bookcases are what structure the space: endless shelves loaded to capacity with books and objects, and topped with wooden model boats, dollhouses, enormous glass, or ceramic fish.

Sometimes the most impenetrable mystery can be couched in an absurd question, like "Which came first, the chicken or the egg?" In Sozzi's case, it would be, "Which came first, the book or the bookcase?" Most likely, the book wins out. Reading matter is what matters most, but then one needs a place to place those books. In stacks, in columns, in vertical piles that resemble heaps of luggage. One book reminds Sozzi of another.

"A book always gives me a broader view of life and of the world," he says. "I don't have time to run around seeing everything that is happening or has happened on the planet, but a single book can take me everywhere."

He rakes through his bookshelves the way others rake their gardens. The book is a tool for understanding the world, an integral part of the reader's living environment: for a designer of Sozzi's caliber, reading also means the physical pleasure of touching and turning the page—a tactile pleasure that he can discuss for hours, just like the feel of fabrics. In fact, the sensations are comparable—a few milligrams of pressure on the fingertips.

Books and more books: Sozzi has designed quite a few himself. Until 2009 he ran a publishing house called RSE, which produced works such as *Metamorfosi*, a marvelous photographic album by Sozzi's friend **Mario de Biasi,** with a preface by Vittorio Sgarbi. A veritable technicolor kaleidoscope, *Metamorfosi* is a series of visual fantasies in which glass, anise blossoms, wood, eggplants, seeds, flowers, and nature itself are broken up into exultant prismatic images. RSE also released *Romeo Sozzi Messaggi*, featuring photographs by Silke Lauffs, a numbered limited edition that depicted most of his furniture creations photographed in sepia or soft focus, backlit or overexposed, refuting the idea that the modernity of his style derives from color, and revealing the importance of material.

Sozzi is no longer in the publishing business, but he does revive books that have faded from memory. One example is the small handbook entitled *L'Arte di Dirigere il Personale e le Officine*, fifty exercises to learn the art of managing an office and its personnel. Published in Turin in 1935 by Professor Luigi Lavagnolo, this curiosity was long out of print until Sozzi found a copy in a used bookshop and had it reprinted just for himself and as a gift for friends. An avid fan of the **Adelphi** series (he owns the entire collection), as well as the comic genius of Laurel & Hardy and the Italian comedian Totò, he especially likes books that make him smile and laugh. Most recently these include *The Evolution Man, Once Upon an Ice Age, What We Did to Father* by Roy Lewis, and *Il Dott. Ciro Amendola, Direttore Della Gazzetta Ufficiale* by Alfonso Celotto. Having grown up with Dante and Simenon, Sozzi the reader adores Voltaire, which seems perfectly appropriate for a chair designer. Perhaps ironically, his own office chair did not spring from his drawing board. In sculpted wood, decorated with gold leaf and mounted on casters, it was discovered in a London antique store and would not look stylistically out of place in a period

[p. 114] ⟶

◆ MARIO DE BIASI, FRIEND AND PHOTOGRAPHER

Gianni Berengo-Gardin and Mario De Biasi are the two Italian photojournalists whose work Romeo Sozzi admires most. In fact, De Biasi, the great maestro of Italian photography, was also a friend until his death in 2013, a few days short of his ninetieth birthday. A national treasure, winner of every prestigious prize and award, he was born in the Veneto region (in Sois, near Belluno) in 1923 and moved to Milan in 1938. Deported to Germany during the war, De Biasi documented the destruction of Nuremberg in 1944, after finding a miraculously undamaged camera in the ruins of the Bavarian city. Back in Milan, he started working as a freelance photojournalist in 1948, chronicling life in post-war Milan—a city ravaged by suffering but imbued with hope—in black and white. In 1953 he was noticed and hired by *Epoca*, the Italian equivalent of *Life* magazine in the United States. He remained with the publication for thirty years, covering a vast range of subjects including the Budapest uprising of 1956; explorer Walter Bonatti's Siberian expedition of 1962 (at temperatures as low as -85 degrees); and the opulent wedding of the Shah of Iran and Farah Diba. Like Doisneau, De Biasi had a knack for catching lovers exchanging a kiss on a park bench, or, like Sam Levin and Roger Corbeau, for capturing the personalities of stars, from Sophia Loren to a very young Claudia Cardinale, from Brigitte Bardot to Andy Warhol. But he earned his place in the annals of twentieth-century photography with an image of a star who wasn't posing, and in fact was walking away. Entitled *Gli Italiani si Voltano (the Italians turn around)*, this black-and-white shot of the circus queen Moira Orfei, taken outside Milan's Galleria Vittorio Emanuele II, on the Duomo side in front of the historic Caffè Zucca, became the poster for *The Italian Metamorphosis 1943–1968*, an exhibition organized by Germano Celant at the Guggenheim in New York in 1994. Honored and exhibited in Arles, Cologne, and Tokyo, Mario De Biasi contributed to many artistic initiatives, like the creation of the Fondazione Forma in Milan, and published more than ninety books in his lifetime. One of his friends, the poet-designer Bruno Munari (inventor of the *chair for a very short visit*—featuring an inclined seat), wrote that De Biasi's camera was part of his body, like his nose and eyes, and that when he wasn't taking photos, the photographer spent his time drawing and painting.

◆ ADELPHI: BOOKS FOR BOOK LOVERS

Founded in Milan in 1962, at a time when the Lombard capital was a thriving hub of the publishing world, Adelphi immediately began releasing masterly novels, essays, and short stories by authors who were not yet known to the general public. In addition to high editorial quality, Adelphi's popularity advanced through the portal of its spare, monochromatic covers, not unlike those of the well-known French publishing house NRF. As the collections proliferated with *Classici, Saggi, gli Adelphi*, and *Piccola Biblioteca* (paperbacks), so did the authors: Adelphi published Ennio Flaiano, Carlo Emilio Gadda, and the provocatively controversial Aldo Busi, while introducing Italian readers to the works of Faulkner, Hesse, Cioran, and Simenon, along with Joseph Roth, Roy Lewis, Ian Fleming (whose oeuvre was not limited to James Bond thrillers), Bruce Chatwin (who gave Moleskine notebooks their place in history), and Paul Scheerbart, the German writer whose treatise *Architettura di Vetro (Glass Architecture)* is one of Romeo Sozzi's bedside books.

film. To make it his own, he upholstered it in bronze silk velvet. That's where he sits, where he writes, sketches, and drafts his designs. His desk is a ship ready to sail, loaded with papers and soft-covered notebooks, as well as folders, boxes, cases, chock-full pencil holders, and bottles of Japanese Iroshisuku Pilot ink for fancy writing.

A few of his pens and mechanical pencils are neatly aligned in a shallow purple platter and **OMAS·** is his favorite, even though the plump Louis Vuitton fountain pen is very much his style. Then there's the Montblanc 12B mechanical pencil with the little emerald-colored stone in the clip, which he always carries with him. Ensconced at this desk, deeper than it is wide, Sozzi takes notes, blackens the pages of his notebook—writing, not jotting; drawing, not doodling—and composes letters. A conscientious correspondent, he sends out many thank-you notes, signed, when the degree of familiarity warrants, with his first name. Romeo: the o serving as a period, signed in red ink (*sanguigna*) with a stroke of pale-blue pastel stick. Need-less to say, those who receive these missives store them with reverent care. In short, Sozzi never stops writing and designing. For him it's an innate need to be fulfilled everywhere, all the time. With no apparent effort, between two topics of conversation, he sketches an idea for a table with three bronze legs and a glass top. His desk is just a pretext that allows him to freely daydream.

"I'll probably think about it tomorrow when I wake up," he says, "and decide to use wool velvet so the glass doesn't slip."

◆ OMAS: PENS FROM
THE FOUNTAIN OF INGENUITY

Dyed in the ink of luxury and pure inventiveness since its founding in Bologna in 1925, Officina Meccanica Armando Simoni, better known under the acronym OMAS, started out as a maker of finely-wrought fountain pens with imaginative extras, like the famous *Penna del Dottore* (doctor's pen) integrating a tiny mercury thermometer, for checking a fever with one end while writing a prescription with the other.

Having inscribed OMAS in the collective consciousness, Simoni conceived other ingenious inventions like the three-pointed pen: nib, ballpoint, and mechanical pencil all in one. Embracing streamlined modernity with the Ogiva and Paragon models, OMAS has never crossed artisanal craftsmanship off its list of values, and continues to produce sleekly elegant pens that are collected and wielded by connoisseurs of premium writing instruments.

As a historical aside, besides being the favorite of Gabriele D'Annunzio, the company was proud to provide the pen, an OMAS 557F, that the twelve member states of the European Union used to sign the Maastricht Treaty on February 7, 1992.

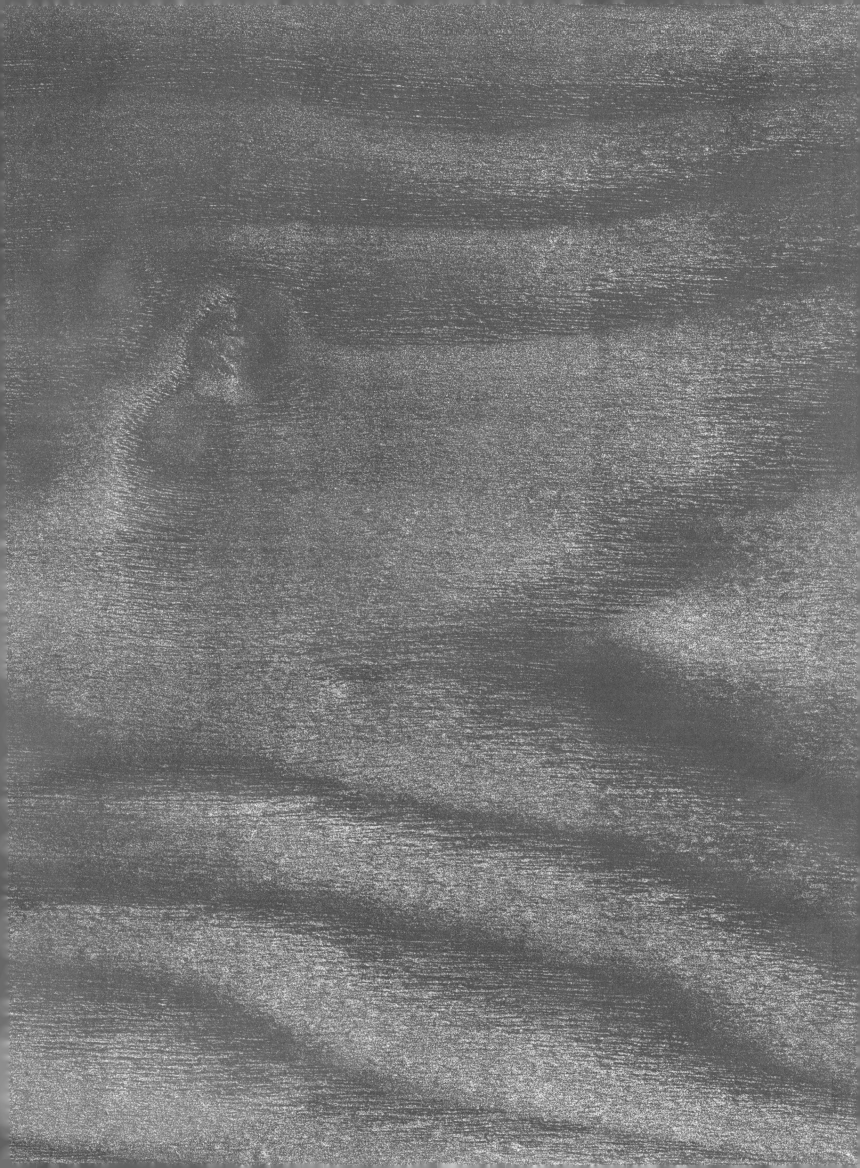

THE EMBLEMS
OF HOSPITALITY

"The real Amphitryon is the Amphitryon with whom we dine," declares the slave Sosia in *Amphitryon*, a play written by the Roman author Plautus (254–184 BCE). Immortalized by this comedy and others by Molière and Jean Giraudoux, Amphitryon descended from the gods and his pedestal to become a common noun officially defined in the Latin languages as "a host who invites guests for a meal." And now from *Comoediae Plautinae* to *Como-ediae Romeosinae*, or rather from Sosia to Sozzi. In charades it's a challenge, and in Scrabble, with those two z's, it's a surefire high score. Indeed, Romeo Sozzi is an amphitryon in the true sense of the term. A gourmet and a gastronome, he loves to invite friends for a drink or a meal, to treat them to the treats that he has personally discovered and carefully selected. Sozzi is a superlative host. In his hands, even a homemade pasta dish becomes a feast. Lunch or dinner with him, at his home, is an enchanting experience, never the same twice, with a *brio* that lends soul to the tomatoes and wit to the zucchini blossoms. Always on the lookout for the finest ingredients, he loves nothing more than to share them, ensuring that everyone goes home with a light heart and a heavy shopping bag.

Sozzi may decorate the world's most beautiful homes, furnishing them with his most refined creations, but his favorite room remains the kitchen, a center of pleasure and companionship, a space made for sharing—even if it's a sumptuous room carved from precious woods, tufted in leather, knobbed in bronze, and surfaced in marble. Like the kitchen in the Angelina showroom in Milan, or the one in the Valmadrera atelier, it is so lavish it could make any multi-starred, multi-stoved chef simmer with envy. For Sozzi, it's merely an innocent way of enhancing the concept of the plain but nourishing lunch, bringing his guests into his world, if only to share a plate of thinly-sliced cold cuts. Magic wand or magic fork? The chefs on hand set happily to work. Their ebullience is infectious: all smiles and eager appetites, the diners savor the offerings of a host for whom the nose, the eye, and the palate are one. Following the example of a man who gives character to a simple panini (simple, perhaps, but made of the best bread and the most flavorful cheese), everyone enters gourmet mode, aided by an atmosphere in which the smallest side dish is

served as though it were a lobster. Colorful leather patchwork placemats as large as the blotter on an ambassador's desk, outsized plates, finely embroidered pure linen napkins—even a quick meal thrown together between two meetings looks like a royal picnic, after which guests are loath to leave the table, lingering over a second cup of coffee just to prolong this unique interlude.

In Milan, at home, or in the Angelina kitchen, stellar Italian cuisine from top chefs enthralls foreign guests, who are delighted to discover such gustatory authenticity and fellowship, while the Italian diners beam with pride, pleased to see how the best of Italy makes visitors from Russia, the United States, or Asia feel right at home. In another setting, this could be called an embassy. To these feasts, exalted by their intrinsic ingenuousness (what could be humbler than rigatoni with cauliflower), never succumbing to fads, Sozzi lends the indispensable touch of a table laid with taste and imagination. Sharing and revelry is paramount, as is making the most elegant silverware part of the fun. To cite one example among many: for a formal dinner at his apartment in Milan after a ballet performance at La Scala, the immense table setting incorporated every imaginable variety of cabbage, arranged in the form of an extraordinary spring garden. Sozzi outdoes Amphitryon: even while leaving nothing to chance, he has a remarkable knack for making it all look improvised, dreamed up at the last minute while waiting for the pasta water to boil. It's a real talent, just like his talent for mixing styles—or people, bringing them together, getting them to talk, laugh, and have fun with each other. And keeping them surprised to the end, with clever little gifts that evoke the themes of the Promemoria collections, the season or the menu itself, like the figurines of *missoltini*, little fish typical of Lake Como, crafted in silver to be worn like a charm on the wrist.

In the kitchen or at the head of the table, from the wine to the pasta, Romeo Sozzi wields solidly constructed tastes—logical for a cabinetmaker. He favors whites for a noon apéritif, unveiling a cellar lined with a thousand bottles of the most sought-after labels, vintages, and origins: Châteauneuf-du-Pape, Barbaresco, pinot noir from the Alto Adige... With a knowing grin, he makes a selection, watching for his guest's expression of approval. How about a Barbera d'Asti, the "masons' wine" that has become a heavenly nectar? *In vino veritas*: wine is meant to be drunk and life is too short for half measures (or glasses). He shows the same care in his choice of mineral water, always bottled in glass, preferably Fiuggi or

Bracca— waters with proven qualities. The former comes from a thermal spring in the Lazio region and the latter is a certified spring water that bubbles forth near Bergamo. Both are excellent restoratives for those who have overdone it at the table. On the bar nestled in the back of his office in Valmadrera, bottles of water stand shoulder-to-shoulder with tubes of vitamins, jars of royal jelly, and various effervescent items of necessity.

But Sozzi's preferred tipple is still the **dry martini,** the subtle alchemy of gin and vermouth that he sips with a conspiratorial smirk, which turns into a smile when a guest follows his lead and renounces champagne, a wine that leaves him cold. Bubbly is not his cup of tea, unlike pasta, a topic on which he waxes enthusiastic, conjuring up piquant images when he asserts that his recipe for *spaghetto* with garlic, olive oil, and red pepper is his absolute favorite dish. Unless it's rigatoni with pepper and Tabasco—an onslaught of flavor, rustic yet heightened by spicy heat. More lenient on the tongue but more laborious to prepare is his *spaghetto al sugo di pomodoro*. It may sound extremely ordinary, but his sauce is a culinary tour de force, a fine-tuned blend of fresh, cherry and pear-shaped Perino tomatoes. Delicious! And sprinkled with parmesan? "Never! Parmesan is heresy! People have been excommunicated for less than that!" Very much in his element with pasta, Sozzi never speaks of spaghetti, but rather spaghetto. The singular, robust, masculine form of the word, due not to any subconscious machismo but in reference to his favorite "make and model" of pasta: Cocco brand *spaghetto antico*, size 0.3, cooking time eight minutes, stirring from time to time with a wooden spoon, *grazie*. A century-old artisanal company based in Fara San Martino in the Abruzzo region, Giuseppe Cocco makes the best *grano duro* dry pasta in Italy. Sozzi treats Cocco pasta like a national treasure, offering an assortment to his foreign friends just as a traditional Italian godfather would do for his boys in the military. As the designer likes to say, "Spaghetto is the cultural link that defines and defends Italian-ness in the world."

The other Italianissimo link that Sozzi upholds every year is his famous Christmas **panettone,** a Milanese classic. He has made it a habit—in fact an unwavering ritual—to send one in an enormous gift box to all of his friends and clients. A symbol of sharing, panettone à la Sozzi is a masterpiece in yeast, flour, and candied fruit, and a pretext for a flavorful afternoon snack in the Promemoria showrooms every December, when Sozzi goes on the road, to Paris, London, New York, and

[p. 137] ⟶

THE DRY MARTINI,
THE PERFECT COCKTAIL, SAYS ROMEO SOZZI

Nicknamed "the elixir of quietude," the dry martini was long a symbol of American modernity, like the Chrysler AirFlow, the Twentieth Century Limited luxury train, and the skyscrapers of Manhattan. In recent years it has come back into fashion and is sipped in chic cocktail bars around the world—notwithstanding countless variations, sometimes bordering on the bizarre.

The object of an imperishable cult in the English-speaking countries, the dry martini cocktail (or gin martini) is thought to have been invented in San Francisco in 1862 by a bartender called "Professor" Jerry Thomas for a prospector who was headed for the mining town of Martinez, California. The ruffian burst into Thomas's bar at the Occidental Hotel bellowing that he wanted "something special!" In those days bartending was a serious business, especially considering that loud, rowdy customers were also likely to be armed. Thomas whipped up a mixture of bitters, maraschino, sweet vermouth, gin and ice, garnished with a slice of lemon. A stiff drink to be sure, which the miner gulped down—and liked so much that he dubbed it the "Martinez." If he had been going to Siskiyou, the name probably would not have caught on.

Another legend, also set against the feverish backdrop of the gold rush, holds that in 1870 a barman named Julio Richelieu at the saloon in Martinez (there it is again) improvised a blend of gin and vermouth with an olive, in an effort to satisfy a thirsty patron who was not happy with the only brand of gin on hand that day—a stopgap solution, in other words. A third version of the story puts the drink's origin in Britain, where the word *martini* was supposedly derived from Martini & Henry, a brand of rifles used between 1871 and 1891 by British soldiers, who compared the as-yet-nameless cocktail to their weapons because both had a reputation for being lethal. Add to these accounts a paternity enthusiastically assumed by the Italian vermouth brand Martini & Rossi, which also dates back to the late nineteenth century, and we see why it's easier to be a martini hound than a martini historian. Another bone of contention: it is thought that a cherry was originally used to embellish the preparation, before being supplanted by the green olive or the twist of lemon. Even the latter detail fiercely divides the purists, with the pro-olive camp torn asunder by its own internal schism: stuffed or unstuffed? And that's not all: when a pickled onion is plopped into a martini it becomes a Gibson. Ultimately, having tried them all for purposes of comparison, no one is able to impose any one variation as definitive, leading to ever-more disputes and slurs of both character and speech.

The term *cocktail* came into common use in Europe in the early 1920s, popularized by early champions of the genre like the Savoy in London, starting in 1910, followed a year later by Harry's New York Bar and the Ritz in Paris. *The Savoy Cocktail Book*, published in 1930, offered two martini recipes: the dry martini cocktail (gin, dry vermouth, and orange bitters) and the martini cocktail (two-thirds gin, one-third vermouth, no orange bitters). Eventually, the expression *dry martini* came to mean any and all cocktails made with dry vermouth, including variations like the Manhattan, the cosmopolitan, and even the Negroni, which was invented in Florence. A thoroughly modern drink, the dry martini paradoxically owed a great deal to Prohibition in the United States. When bootlegged whisky became undrinkably bad, more and more tipplers turned to gin, and along with it all of the derived concoctions, whose transparency was a sign of quality as well as elegant simplicity. Roosevelt drank it with a dollop of anisette and Hemingway insisted that it be made with fifteen parts gin to one part dry vermouth. The scathing gossip columnist Walter Winchell nicknamed Robert Benchley, Anita Loos, and the other famous writers who frequented New York's Algonquin Hotel the "Gintellectuals." Acknowledging the martini's powerful ability to break down inhibitions, Dorothy Parker trenchantly (and truthfully) wrote:

> "I like to have a martini,
> Two at the very most.
> After three I'm under the table,
> After four I'm under my host."

It was a time when martini lunches were all the rage. In *Our Modern Maidens*, a silent film from 1929, a modern society lady played by a very young Joan Crawford announces to her guests, via title card: "Dinner is poured!" Fabulous. In the movies, the decidedly photogenic dry martini instantly gave any character an air of well-heeled elegance, while the darker yellow and brown brews identified their drinkers as denizens of the low dive and the gutter. Only (faux) champagne could outclass gin. On the big screen the dry martini was a mainstay for Frank Sinatra and Dean Martin, and every film buff can recite Bette Davis's classic line from *All About Eve*: "I'd like a martini, very dry . . . Fasten your seatbelts, it's going to be a bumpy night." But of course it was James Bond who made the martini the ultimate cocktail. In Ian Fleming's 1953 novel *Casino Royale*, Agent 007 uttered these earthshaking words: "A dry martini . . . In a deep champagne goblet . . . Three measures of Gordon's, one of vodka, half a measure of Kina Lillet. Shake it very well until it's ice cold, then add

a large thin slice of lemon peel. Got it?" The cornerstone and lifeblood of the Bond legend, on par with his Aston Martin, this martini is nonetheless a sacrilege to purists because: vodka is out of the question, and the shaker alters the molecular structure of the gin. Which means that the whole "shaken-not-stirred" business is just a lot of hot air.

In the 1960s, the most popular wedding gift in the US and the UK was the martini set. The dry martini, described with catchy oxymorons like "sensuous coldness" and "opulent dryness," can only be served in a proper martini glass, with a V-shaped bowl on a long slim stem, compared rather grandiloquently to "a ballerina *en pointe*." The glass is a perennial subject of research, resculpted and refined by many a designer. I have investigated the matter myself, making my own formal contribution to this exercise in glassmaking.

The illustrious architect-designer Mies van der Rohe, a proponent of "less is more" and a martini aficionado, considered the martini glass the most finely, delicately balanced object ever made. Another distinguished martini devotee was the Spanish filmmaker Luis Buñuel, who swore by only one of the forty officially accepted methods for preparing the "perfect cocktail," which involved dipping the ice cubes in Noilly Prat vermouth, a trick that is supposed to prevent the ice from melting. As for W. C. Fields, the sardonic comic genius par excellence whose wit I adore, he downed a martini every morning before and after breakfast, which more often than not consisted of a Bloody Mary. *Cha-pe-au!*

Moscow, bearing gifts like the Three Kings. No one would dare miss this mouth-watering event, and no one is ever disappointed that the frankincense and myrrh have been replaced by *mandarini*, *torroni*, and other goodies summoned forth to celebrate the Nativity.

Another ritual beloved by Sozzi is the summer concert that he hosts every July before everyone leaves on vacation, which puts Varenna back on the social calendar and revives a musical tradition that dates back to the nineteenth century, when Countess Campioni Venini brought in orchestras to play on rafts in the middle of the lake so that the music could be heard on both shores. Not quite so extravagant, Sozzi makes do with his garden or his stretch of the lakeshore, playing impresario for a voice and piano recital, inviting an actress friend to declaim D'Annunzio, or hiring a jazz group to jam the night away.

There's a dress code, more for fun than formality that everyone obeys with good cheer and even anticipation in the warm summer night. Romeo Sozzi offhand-edly mentions another musical idea, but knowing our man it's more than an idle thought: "I dream of organizing concerts in the cloister of the Cistercian abbey of Piona in Colico, not far from Lecco. It's a thirteenth-century building designed by Bonaccorso da Gravedona in a pure Romanesque-Lombard style—sublime—I get goose bumps just talking about it!"

PANETTONE,
AMORE AND FANTASY

A typically Milanese specialty and a symbol of the year-end holiday season all over Italy, the panettone dates back to the Renaissance. Like *risotto giallo*, aka *risotto alla milanese*, its origins are explained by two different legends, both accepted as gospel. According to the first story, a pastry chef in the employ of Ludovico il Moro, lord of Milan, was seeking inspiration for a dessert to serve at a banquet when one of his underlings seized the opportunity to propose a kind of bread that he had improvised, enriching the dough with sugar, butter, raisins, citron zest, and candied orange, plus a hefty extra dose of yeast. It was a brash move, straying from the master's formulas—in those days people were hanged for less. But once it was baked, the bread, light, and voluminous, puffed up with so much yeast, proved delicious. The members of the court licked their fingers clean (and no doubt wiped their hands on the curtains). The recipe was duly recorded, rewarded, and copied. And named: from *pan grande* to *panettone* ("big bread") the transition took only a few tastes before it was digested and approved. The second legend, a bit shorter and harder to swallow, operates on the hypothesis that panettone started life as *pan di Ton*, "Ton" being the name of the pastry chef on duty that day, in the kitchens of that same lord, and who cooked up the first loaf of big bread. And *basta!*

Whatever its actual genesis, the panettone was promoted to the status of traditional Christmas cake in Lombardy, later to be enshrined as an institution, and even a high-stakes political symbol when Metternich tried to appease the Milanese after the famous *Cinque Giornate* (Five Days) of revolt against Austrian-Hungarian rule by distributing a poster that showed him holding a panettone in each arm. A clever ploy, but it soon went stale: his panettone were not the real thing. Industrialized by Motta in the early twentieth century, panettone became an unassailable Italian national emblem. Scorning the mass-produced version, today's Milanese vie with each other to find the best panettone made by genuine pastry chefs, 100 percent artisanal down to the smallest morsels of candied fruit, to be eaten between Christmas (give or take a few days) and February 3, the Feast of San Biagio. True connoisseurs have a golden rule: never order or buy a panettone that weighs less than a kilogram (two pounds), which is considered the ideal weight for good conservation and the sanctioned minimum for a respectable holiday gift. More than two kilos (just over four pounds) is an overdose—not to mention the aesthetic shortcomings of a cake that looks more like an ottoman. Every year before Christmas, Romeo Sozzi orders hundreds of panettone to give to friends, customers, and journalists. It has become a tradition that he would never dream of forgoing.

COLLECTOR

◆

a person who
enjoys collecting

^A COLLECTOR ^{OF} COLLECTIONS

"A person who enjoys collecting." The origins of Romeo Sozzi's *collectionary* tendencies are to be found in this definition and its verb, enjoy, rather than in any psychological profile hastily extrapolated from a few scholarly observations. Sigmund Freud, who collected some 2,000 relics of various extinct Mediterranean civilizations, along with a few Chinese antiquities of dubious authenticity, refrained from analyzing the impulse—he who said "good morning" every day to a squat Chinese figurine on his desk. Before that, every Wednesday for thirty years Freud made the rounds of the Viennese antique dealers to expand his collection, which, he said, afforded him great relaxation. Nonetheless, the psychiatric clan would have gladly offered a diagnosis: collecting reflects the desire to possess, the need for spontaneous activity, a striving to surpass oneself, and a penchant for classification.

One might also add an intellectual possessiveness. As for the collector, he is a zealous being who revels in the exploration, appreciation, and dedication involved, in both the short and long term. Behind the collector's passion lies a concern for beauty, aestheticism, and order that supplies the inertia needed to confront impermanence, in particular of trends and fashions. The collector grants himself the privilege of a stable benchmark and in this sense, the collection neutralizes any potential disorder.

The act of collecting is also considered a form of narcissistic reinforcement: a good collector is a well-informed, perspicacious person, resolutely determined in his investigations and procedures. He nurtures a genuine pride in his obsession, cultivating all related knowledge to its fullest and committing himself to the protection of a cultural heritage. According to the Bible, Noah was the first collector—in his case to save lives and preserve biodiversity. Those who followed, more or less famous, would bequeath their collections to subsequent generations as an inheritance or endowment. The moral of the story: without collectors, large or small, there would be no museums, no galleries, no foundations. Prestigious or not, if they had never been collected, no toys, tools, artifacts, or artworks would have ended up in museum exhibits. As for the collection itself, regardless of its focus and content, it is, by nature, never completed. And the collector, narcissistic or not, never stops collecting—although he might start collecting something else or pursue multiple

COLLECTION

◆

From the Latin *collectio*.
An assemblage of objects chosen
for their beauty, personal
value, monetary value,
or documentary interest

collections, with or without thematic links, and with no need to offer any explanation for such versatility. In fact, with any type of collection, every object in it has a special meaning to which the collector attaches a fervor diametrically opposed to its rarity, its value, its market price, or its origin. Consequently, "collector's syndrome," although easy to analyze as a psychological projection, is neither a pathological behavior nor a disease: it is a treatment unto itself, with self-prescribed and self-administered doses.

According to the French writer Maurice Rheims, a member of the Académie Française and a brilliant auctioneer, *"The taste for collecting is a game of passion."* The author of many books on the subject, including *The Strange Life of Objects* and *Les Collectionneurs*, Rheims knew what he was talking about. As did Jean Baudrillard: an early theorist of postmodernity, this philosopher, fascinated with the phenomena of simulacra and hyperreality in mass media, examined the psychological motives that impel people to amass collections, and expressed his conclusion in terms of the object of passion, the beloved object. Previously, he had described how a simple object, stripped of its function or detached from its practical purpose, acquires a strictly subjective status by becoming an object in a collection. And how subsequently, a single object is no longer enough: a collection is always a series of objects whose totality is the primary goal. Baudrillard went on to propose the idea that collecting is a pastime in the sense of exerting control over time, and that devoting oneself to a collection helps control the world and control time by suspending it and categorizing it in the same mode as behavioral habits.

More prosaically, a collector like Romeo Sozzi sees his collections as an affirmation of his freedom of taste, a channel for expressing his uniqueness, as well as his eccentricities, flouting bureaucratic structures, defying the burdens of everyday life, and the constraints of the immediate present. A true collector, he knows everything there is to know about his collections and the objects in them. And like all collectors who know that they are defined by what they collect, as soon as his collection becomes known, if only within a closed circle, he acknowledges the fact and makes an effort to turn that collection into a social and sociable factor, a framework for rituals and performances. In fact, Sozzi is a collector of collections: well-known for his collection of frogs (and for using a frog as the emblem of Promemoria), he also collects vintage cars and motorcycles, film cameras, twentieth-century designer furniture, outsider and primitive art objects, books, pens, and inks. All are obsessions that he considers, as Baudrillard would have said, pastimes, knowing that there is nothing sacred about them. Most of his collections start from something trivial: a memory, a gift, a chance find in a flea market or an antiques shop. They don't make him an authority sought out by experts. Sozzi's collections meet personal, informal criteria, not museum standards. Everything that he collects is put to use, and the restoration work carried out on his antique cars and motorcycles is not for the purpose of making them show-worthy, but simply to revive the beauty and pleasure of the original vehicle.

HIS FROG COLLECTION

Romeo Sozzi started collecting frogs long before he began drawing them, turning them into his emblem, then doorstops, and later candles. Everyone who knows him knows about his frog collection, which makes it easy for friends to find gifts and greeting cards that are sure to make him smile. At home, at the atelier or in his office, in Milan or Varenna, his frogs make up a sort of miniature amphibian theme park, including spring-powered specimens in plastic, fabric, or knits that jump blithely from a tabletop to a chair, while others peek out from behind the cushions of a sofa, undermining any semblance of decorative decorum. From his sketchpad there has evolved a web-footed mascot, the Sozzi Frog, a new species not yet known to the biological sciences, but nonetheless symbolic: since ancient times, the frog has been the subject of allegory and legend. Its intrinsic metamorphosis from tadpole to adult makes it synonymous with resurrection. A nourishing totem since antiquity, a benevolent little spirit close to God when He reigned over water, the frog wins the prize for fertility. According to Vietnamese tradition, while the body sleeps the soul moves about in the form of a frog, and in the West, once upon a time, all it took to turn a frog into a charming prince was a kiss from a princess with a pure heart. The Grimm Brothers' Frog King, La Fontaine's bullfrog who wanted to be bigger than an ox, the weather frog, the star of *The Muppet Show*… They can all be found in Sozzi's frog pond.

The designer has his own pet theory: the frog, having jumpy nerves, always leaps forward and never moves backwards. A trajectory—a green trajectory. The litera-

ture, fables, folk tales, and memories of life science class… Sozzi knows them all by heart. His cheapest frog is plastic with hinged legs, and his most precious is made of gold. Then there are the inevitable candles, the Kermit PC screen, the crowned plush toys. His own frogs, forged in bronze from 1999, do double duty as doorstops and good luck charms. "I found out that that was how they are used in Central Europe, in China, and Japan as well." As a result, more than 300 of them can be found frolicking all over the house, from the barometer to the bathroom tiles, plus a bit of big-mouthed-frog bombast. Instead of lily pads, we have gray delivery trucks adorned with the graphic silhouette of the Sozzi Frog, always jumping forward.

VINTAGE VEHICLES

There are hints everywhere, like the miniature motorcycle in driftwood and rusted iron parked against a wall of the staircase leading to his office in the Valmadrera atelier. A mere decorative toy compared with the black, silver, and khaki motorcycle leaning on its kickstand outside—an ultra-modern, muscular beast of a bike.

When he doesn't want to travel by car, Romeo Sozzi dons his helmet and rides hell bent for leather on two wheels. His bikes are parked in a garage flanked by an engine shop with enough tools to make any grease monkey green with envy. Not long ago, his son Davide, who is as equally passionate for Vespa and English bikes, finished restoring a splendid 1950 Norton ES2. The project took an entire year, and for good reason: every single part, from the handlebars to the wheel hubs, from the bolts to the suspension cylinders, from the headlight housing to the fuel tank cap, was cast in bronze! Romeo and Davide Sozzi also own a white BMW GS 1000 and a 1972 Ducati Scrambler. "I have ridden them all and I still ride them today. And they do make a racket!"

On a quieter note, Sozzi also has a fleet of vintage bicycles, including a Swedish Kronan, a Belgian Gazelle, a blue Italian baker's bike, and an Atlas with rod brakes. But the most curious items in this freewheeling collection are a Bianchi Aquilotto, a 50cc moped from the 1950s with a special feature: the engine can be removed to transform it from motorbike to a bicycle, and a Moto Guzzi Galletto, a streamlined, pale yellow single-seat scooter with the spare tire mounted on the

front of the leg guard. It's the first motorized two-wheeler that Sozzi bought and rode as a young man. A prized scooter and very well-preserved, aided by the fact that the Moto Guzzi company, founded in 1921, is located on the lake, in Mandello del Lario about a mile from Lecco. A cult brand if ever there was one, Moto Guzzi, with its flying eagle logo, has produced legendary machines (the California, the Guzzino 65, the V7 Sport, the Norge 1200) that have held every racetrack record, and is still in high gear as part of the Piaggio Group, with a loyal following of thousands of *Guzzisti*.

His first car was an Autobianchi Bianchina Panoramica, sky blue with a black roof, a tiny station wagon modeled after the elfin Bianchina, which in turn was modeled after the Fiat 500. It ran on recycled used oil.

Romeo Sozzi loves cars, and speed. He loves their power and the beauty of their engine, body, and paint job. He likes Jaguars, particularly the 1962 E-Type that he restored. One of the great legends of automotive history, a British road rocket designed by Malcolm Sayer and made in Coventry, the E-Type, or XKE, came from Series 1, the most sought-after by car buffs. Its original color was opalescent silver blue, but it later appeared in cobalt blue and then black, like the one owned by Diabolik, the evil antihero of the cult Italian comic strip of the same name, perhaps not coincidentally launched in 1962 by two Milanese sisters, Angela and Luciana Giussani. At the time, another XKE was in the Italian pop culture spotlight: the pink one owned by the red-haired singer Rita Pavone, nicknamed La Zanzara. Sozzi's vintage car collection also includes a praline beige VW Beetle 1300 DeLuxe, nicknamed the "Maggiolino" or "Maggiolone" in Italy. "This Beetle belonged to a Promemoria customer who traded it for a piece of furniture. I accepted the deal because I wanted to give the car to my son Davide. Its owner, a very chic lady, swore that her Volkswagen was

"When I bought this E-Type, it only had 70,000 kilometers (approx. 43,000 miles) on the odometer and was running perfectly. It had belonged to a physician that had a collection of thirty sports cars and a hundred motorcycles. He had kept his Jaguar in perfect condition in the garage —a collector's dream!"

in impeccable condition, and, knowing my passion for cars, she knew that it would be well taken care of. It was her husband who delivered it, parking it in front of my office. And then, just like Herbie in Disney's *Love Bug* movies, the VW threw a fit and ruptured its crankcase: I found it sitting in a pool of oil."

Although many of Sozzi's cars have come and gone, including a Land Rover which he had upholstered with white linen for an expedition to the Sahara, and above all a magnificent red 1963 Facel Vega Facellia III (with a Volvo engine), he has kept his Mercedes-Benz 190 SL convertible, body and engine painstakingly restored. Silver on the outside, with a vermillion leather interior, a white bakelite steering wheel, and a black hood, this roadster, whose speedometer goes up to 105 mph for a reason, was made between 1955 and 1963, with a total production run of 25,881. Driven by Frank Sinatra in *Ten Thousand Bedrooms* and Barbara Sukowa in R. W. Fassbinder's *Lola*, the 190 SL was launched to offer the American market a more economical version of the stunning 300 SL with gull-wing doors.

Between two raised hoods and three twists of the ignition, just to listen to the music of the engines, Sozzi dreams of one day owning a 1952 Bentley R Continental Coupe, if possible in two-tone green and silver. A holy grail for car collectors, with a streamlined fastback body sculpted in a wind tunnel and produced by the illustrious coachbuilder H. J. Mulliner & Co., it was in its day the fastest four-seater in the world. Only 250 were made, 207 with right-hand drive and 43 with the wheel on the left.

Meanwhile, Sozzi is finishing the restoration of an unusual American car: a 1948 Ford V8 Super DeLuxe "woodie." Yes, a car with a wooden body: what happens when carpenter meets car designer. Originally licensed in Utah and purchased in London, this stately station wagon, weighing 1.6 tons, represents a formerly popular American genre: cars with posts and panels made of varnished wood, designed for hunters and outdoorsmen, heirs to the luxurious boat-shaped wooden touring cars of the twenties and thirties. Besides station wagons, woodie convertibles were also seen as stylish, like the Chrysler Town & Country, and the Ford Sportsman. With a production run of 9,000, the Super DeLuxe was available in two different finishes, maple or birch, with maple accounting for 90 percent of the sales. Sozzi has gone one better, restoring his woodie with a body frame, posts, and panels in mahogany. Like the Riva motorboat, for Sozzi this odd-looking Ford is a finely crafted, mobile piece of furniture.

HIS CAMERAS

When Romeo Sozzi was a young boy, his father gave him an easy-to-use Kodak camera. Later the elder Sozzi gave his son his own Leica, a IIIG from 1939 that would be the starting point of a collection, and then a Hasselblad. The future designer became fascinated with photography, capturing landscapes, making portraits, and studies of female anatomy. The art form turned into a real passion in 1975 after he broke a leg skiing. He had also begun painting by then, but his enforced immobility, just like James Stewart in *Rear Window*, focused his attention on the photograph. He set up his dark room in an unheated studio, where he wore two loden coats to stay warm while working in the winter.

Sozzi didn't buy his own first Leica until 1995, an M4. Then came an M5, and an M6. Having no desire to succumb to digital technology with an M8, he fell back on the human, manual M7. Today he keeps most of his cameras in a cabinet in his Valmadrera office, and others, like his vintage Leicas, at the lake house in Varenna. A great admirer of film photography, with an indelible memory of Gregory Colbert's photos of elephants seen at the Arsenale during the Venice Biennale in 2002, Sozzi is still taking photos—in fact, more than ever, and in black and white. Images of hands or feet against black backgrounds with carefully studied lighting, of tree bark, leaves, and mountainscapes seen during his long hikes in the woods. Photography is his secret world—despite his love of books, he has never published any of his visual work.

HIS FURNITURE STOREHOUSE

Is it really a collection? *Accumulation* might be a better word. In a vast room adjoining his office in Valmadrera and filled with enormous blue tubular structures, Sozzi stacks up and stores pieces of furniture found in stores, antique shops, and flea markets, all out of circulation for the moment, waiting to be brought back to life as sources of inspiration or subjects of restoration. The inventory includes sideboards, writing desks, tables, stools, ottomans, armchairs, wing chairs, cabriole chairs, and voltaire chairs.

Wandering aimlessly through the space we find, in no particular order, a Hans J. Wegner, a white enamel and burgundy leatherette barber's chair, a *Feltri* lounge

chair by Gaetano Pesce for Cassina, a sprawling scarlet leather armchair with wings but no feet, a *Pamio* by Alvar Aalto, an elegant gilded brass "bamboo" bridge chair, and a rattan lounge chair that could well be a Franco Albini/Franca Helg.

As the antechamber to this treasure trove, Sozzi's spacious office seems to have absorbed a few pieces from the storehouse, whose forms are discernable under the heaps of shopping bags and fabrics, the chair backs serving as display stands for framed photographs or paintings. In rattan, leather or straw, a few vintage Italian, French, and Scandinavian chairs are lined up as though waiting to accommodate the visitors who wouldn't dare sit in them—even the Philippe Starck garden gnome stool is occupied by a squadron of multicolored frogs.

Also on duty is a *Bilou Bilou* chair, sheathed in snakeskin, playing the tempter in this design fan's Garden of Eden.

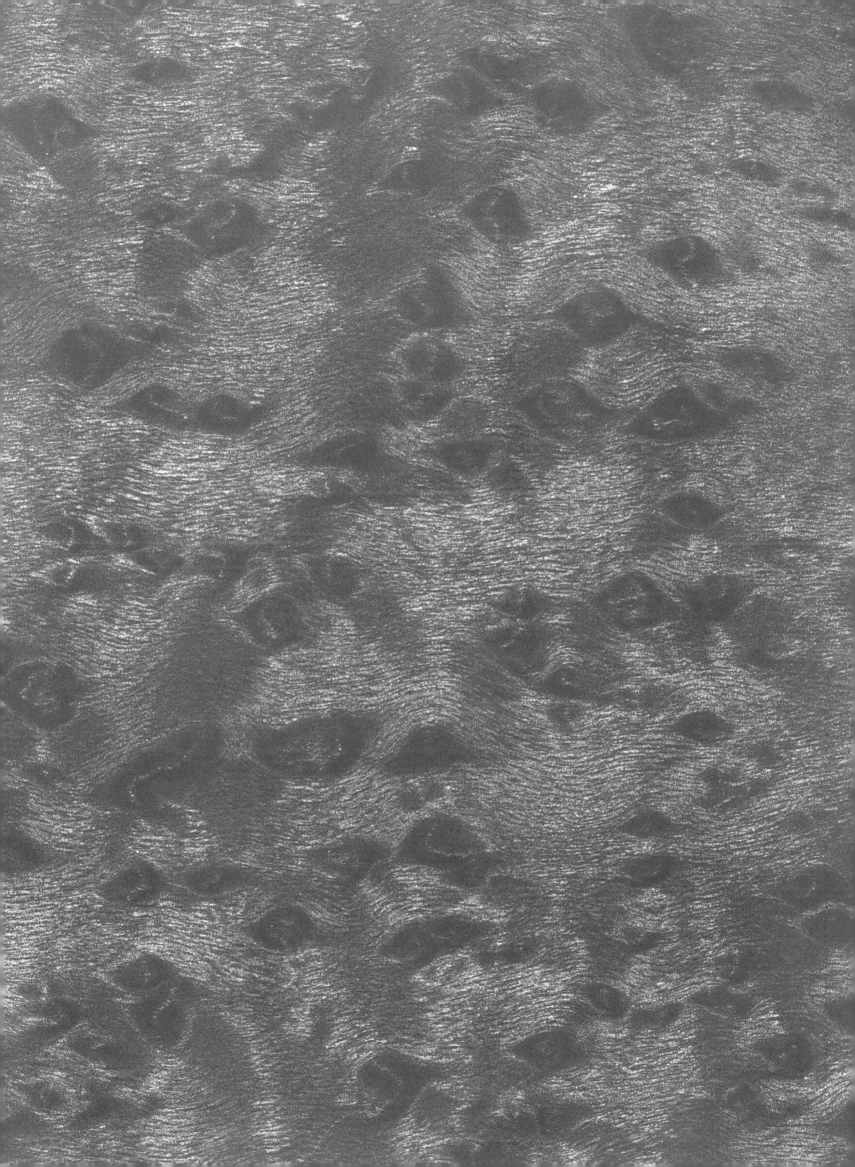

A MULTIFACETED ELEGANCE

Ineffably charming at first glance, with a piercing gaze, and always smiling, always on the go, at ease in all circumstances, Romeo Sozzi does not move from one place to another; he is propelled. Always well groomed, smartly dressed, the orchestrator of his own elegance, he takes pains to evaluate the significance of sartorial symbols and standards, which he then transmutes or transgresses, turning them into benchmarks of his personal style. It's not so much an ability as it is a talent. And it's not at all about being fashionable. Fashion is made to be followed, but he prefers to anticipate it, as long as he sees it as meaningful and worthwhile. There is no artifice in Sozzi's look. His inexhaustible natural energy is metabolized in colors and materials. He follows his fancy from head to toe, and it is in fact with the toes—or rather the feet—that we begin our inventory of his wardrobe.

Signor Sozzi's footwear repertoire walks the line between ankle boots, loafers, wingtips, oxfords, and sneakers. For a motorcycle ride he wears sneakers in the summer and biker boots in the winter, never anything else: "The gearshift wears out all of my left shoes." Not surprisingly, he does not dress his feet in conventional leathers or colors. Crocodile, ostrich, velvet, glazed linen, tartan wool: the material takes the spotlight while the color explores the rainbow. High in appeal and flat in the heel: slippers are his favorite footwear. But not just any slippers: in ribbed velvet, zebra print, evening wear, satin or raffia, embellished with a little emblematic bow… Their name? Belgian Shoes. Both slip-ons and slippers, the Belgian Shoes are handmade in an infinite range of materials and colors accented with contrasting piping. "Signed" with their little signature bow, they can be worn day or night, winter or summer. Silken, velvety, zebra-striped, crimson, in ostrich, lizard, cashmere, raffia, tartan wool, glen check tweed…

When he is not wearing them, Sozzi pampers his shoes. To the point that he has even designed a special shoeshine stand, whose prototype sits in his Valmadrera office. He admits it without the least embarrassment: he loves shining his shoes. Refreshing the color with a cloth dipped in polish, bringing out the sheen and the luster with a brush, and with plenty of elbow grease. Is there any real difference between the cabinetmaker nourishing his wood with a clear varnish and the shoe

shiner burnishing his leather with a natural polish? After all, people and furniture both have feet.

To the parlor game question "If you were a piece of furniture, what would it be?" Sozzi has a ready answer: an armoire. Which is convenient, since he makes armoires himself. The man who makes the armoires that make the man, Sozzi is not, however, built like an armoire. His figure today is the same as when he was younger. Meanwhile, since Sozzi's younger days, the armoire as a genre has lost ground, rendered old-fashioned by built-in closets. Admittedly, an armoire's size does not lend itself to lighthearted fantasy. An armoire is a serious thing. But also comforting: a family heirloom, the cabinet in which Nonna kept her linens, to be handed down to the next generation still filled with the embroidered sheets from her trousseau, the symbol of an orderly household, provided that there is someone to keep the house in order. Both necessary and unique, the armoire inspired the designers of steamer trunks, which became reduced-scale portable dressing rooms. Which leads us to the full-scale dressing room: a small chamber adjoining the bedroom and devoted exclusively to the hanging and storage of clothes. The French borrowed the English term, calling it a *dressing*, or more properly a *cabinet de toilette* or *vestiaire*. In Italian it was a *cabina armadio*.

After World War II the dressing room declined as the cost of dwelling space rose, but lately it has been returning to duty, configured and fitted out as the ultimate bastion of privacy. A few shelves, racks, built-in trays, wheeled sets of drawers, hangers, and mirrored sliding doors: designed to be practical, the basic assemble-it-yourself dressing room suite does not inspire much emotion, whereas the full-blown walk-in version, an entire room, is the stuff of dreams. If only we could install one of those computer-controlled electric carousels that dry cleaners use, to find what we're looking for without having to search for it, it would be nirvana. Although not computerized, the dressing rooms that Sozzi designs for his clients are sumptuous centers of incredible luxury. Modern-day boudoirs, ultra-private sanctums in which anything is possible, decoratively speaking, from special hangers for jackets to special drawers for socks, trays for watches and bracelets, racks for shoes, compartments for cufflinks… It would be easy to spend all day in there—it's nearly a shame to have to get dressed and come out.

For his own extensive wardrobes, Sozzi straddles the best of both worlds, armoire and dressing room. Why limit oneself to a single configuration when there's

space to spare? Suave and sophisticated, Sozzi embraces all forms of finery in style and color. Wielding an ebullient taste for fabrics, juxtaposed with an innate sense of color, he dresses, winter and summer, in a rather unorthodox style for a northern Italian entrepreneur. The artist and the bon vivant outshine the cabinetmaker and business manager, without betraying the collector's intrinsic elegance. In fact, he distills its elusive essence, which becomes the foundation of an instantly recognizable look that is all his own. Nothing eccentric—just an artful, refined mix from a personalized wardrobe in which, in appearance, trousers are still trousers, a shirt is still a shirt, a jacket is still a jacket. The necktie, however, was banished long ago, replaced and outclassed by a spectacular array of scarves, of which he owns dozens and dozens—a genuine repository.

To look through Sozzi's armoires is to compile a sartorial inventory of a man under the influence—of textiles. Perfectly normal for an interior designer, one would think, but Romeo Sozzi has shown himself to be more than that: he is a consummate colorist, capable of devising the most audacious yet harmonious shades, nuances, and combinations. The link is forged between what he designs and what he wears, with an emphasis on the sensory. Regardless of the style— sport or city, casual or evening wear—his textile catalog lists linen, cotton, silk, shantung, wool, velvet, suede, and Loden. As for the color palette, it cheerfully ventures beyond the established ranges, focusing primarily on the trousers, mostly from **Etro,** which serve as the medium of his chromatic creativity. Saffron, anise, coral, violet, Brunswick green, lilac, absinthe, turquoise, dove gray, indigo, bronze, white, cobalt, iridescent blue-gray, linden green, raspberry, chartreuse, royal blue, mustard yellow… It's enough to make a painter drop his jaw and his brush. Sozzi takes them all in stride, remembering to request an adjustment in the size and shape of the back pockets in order to accommodate his ever-present notepad. Otherwise, the right front pocket is reserved for cash and the left for his cardholder. Pant loops for slipping on belts are in sharp colors, highlighting his waist with a thin bright band.

Although by no means a turncoat, Sozzi likes to sport different styles of jacket: a blazer with piping, a hunting jacket, a Forestière with a stand-up collar evoking the Orient, Asia, Austria, or South Tyrol. Here again, the notepads fit smoothly into the pockets. One layer below, his shirts cut a more sedate profile, custom-tailored in white or blue cotton poplin. For striped and patterned shirts he relies, once again, on Etro. In the summer, said shirts will be in crinkled linen, candy colored,

[p.204] ⟶

It all started in 1968. While some people clamored for political revolution, others fomented revolutions in style. Gerolamo Etro did both. Nicknamed Gimmo, this erudite collector of fashion, paintings, and decorative curiosities founded a factory for household textiles on Via Pontaccio, in the heart of the Brera district of Milan. His products immediately caught the eye of the key figures in the new Milanese school of interior design. Silks, linens, cashmeres—and especially his iconic paisley pattern, the composite motif that would forge his reputation and identity, lining the interiors of handbags and suitcases, and later the pockets of trousers. There followed neckties, scarves, shawls, and other accessories. And then shops: in Italy, throughout Europe, and around the world. A new wave of color inundated the fashion world, bringing in looks for men that would make the latest Technicolor blockbuster seem as drab as an old black-and-white silent short. Every runway show was a florid bouquet, allowing stylish men to revel with childlike joy in a rainbow of color. An exemplar of the family-owned fashion house, Etro scored a direct hit with its witty stylings, its fragrances, its *casa* line (home decoration remains a core activity) and above all its color palettes, expressing the most positive attributes of the modern mindset: courage, enthusiasm, desire, mystery, confidence, dynamism, and coolheadedness.

Baule

pastel, or with a Liberty-like floral pattern. And if Sozzi wears it, it will have a breast pocket harboring a fountain pen and/or mechanical pencil, plus a thin crocodile case concealing a pair of reading glasses with eye-catching, colorful frames, from a New York optician on Madison Ave.

Around his wrist, Sozzi casually clasps one of the three watches that he owns. Although he admires complexity in furniture, the complications inherent to watchmaking interest him less. They may have aroused his desire years ago, but his tastes have mellowed with time. Watch-spotters will notice him wearing an IWC chronograph when taking off for a motorcycle ride or a hike in the mountains, or a Vacheron-Constantin: when Romeo's father Felice Sozzi reached his eightieth birthday in 2002, he decided to mark the occasion by giving it to his son. In the back of a drawer he stores two silver pocket watches that belonged to Felice's father, who taught Romeo to appreciate, and lament the demise of, the lovely, old-fashioned gesture of pulling a chain on the front of one's vest to check the time.

A Panama on his head when the sun beats down, sneakers for walking, heavy ankle boots in greased leather for hiking … After starting out on the right (and left) foot, our inventory of Sozzi's wardrobe reverts to shoes, with a mention of the much-admired craftsmanship of **Aubercy,** a Parisian bootmaker that he would gladly make his sole supplier.

Snooping around his house, the nosier-than-usual observer will note the presence of a silent servant. No, it's not a portrait of the faithful Bernardo from *Zorro*, but a valet stand topped with a hanger, a trousers holder, a change tray, and a shoe rack. This assembly can generally be found not far from the bed or in the middle of the dressing room. Some see it as the accoutrement of a fussy old bachelor, a misfit in the age of the jeans wadded up and tossed into a corner, the wrinkle-free suit hanging on a bent nail and the shoes yanked off, still laced, with about as much ceremony as a customs agent ripping open a suspicious package with a pair of pliers. Others see it as the accessory of a man who is enviably attentive to the condition of his personal effects. Invented by the English as a means of preventing wrinkles in their clothes and reputations, the valet is a woodworking exercise that certain furniture makers have turned into a formal and functional manifesto. Like the Valet PP 250, created in 1953 by the illustrious Danish cabinetmaker and designer Hans J. Wegner, a solid pine and teak structure with brass trim to which Sozzi doffs his hat in reverence, paying fealty to a valet.

◆ AUBERCY:
PARISIAN TO THE TOES

One could say that Xavier Aubercy was born in a shoe-box. This exquisitely well-mannered dandy and gourmet, representing the third generation of a dynasty of Parisian bootmakers, is the worthy heir of the know-how handed down from his great-grandfather André Aubercy, who founded the house in 1935, and his father Philippe Aubercy. With 6,000 customers, including many of the most powerful and prominent men of France, the house has two locations: the historic shop on Rue Vivienne, between the old stock exchange and the Right Bank boulevards, and the Left Bank shop on Rue de Luynes, in the exclusive Saint Germain district. The former surrounded by banks and the press, the latter among the literary monuments and ministerial offices. Bespoke, semi-bespoke, or ready-to-wear, the repertoire, classic by necessity, is embellished with touches of unbridled fantasy. The Aubercy avocado green, the "Reverso" stitch, the lustrous "castagna" finish, the flamboyant crocodiles, and the shagreens, famously hard to work with but producing a marble-like surface (sharkskin, although now rare, has at last shed its "prince of the night" connotations), all herald and highlight the lasting talent of an exceptional bootmaker, a purveyor of subtle elegance. Sharing with Xavier Aubercy a dedication to fine craftsmanship and the modesty that goes with maintaining the highest standards, Romeo Sozzi could only leap with both feet into these exquisite shoes.

A PORTRAIT
IN SHADES AND NUANCES

Sozzi. Romeo Sozzi. In the rarefied yet high profile world of interior design and decoration made in Italy and prized around the world, the name is the very definition of contemporary beauty and elegance. A short name that begins with a romantic murmur, *Romeo*, and ends in an emphatic *zzi*, fittingly preceded by an insistent *so*! Pronounced *So-tsee* to flatter his paternal line, but not himself. Indifferent to adulation, Sozzi keeps some facets deliberately hidden.

Sono Sozzi. In Italy, according to custom as well as *il galateo*, the rules of decorum so dear to polite society, one introduces oneself by enunciating the family name first, preceded by sono (I am). In practice, Romeo Sozzi has no need to obey this precept of everyday good manners. Anyone who knows about design knows who he is, even if they have never met. The members of his inner circle refer to **Romeo,** while his employees greet him with a more respectful "Signor Romeo." As for the man himself, he greets his friends and family with a broad smile and outstretched arms. There might follow, depending on the relationship and circumstances, a handshake, cheek kisses, or a hug, but whatever the gesture, it is delivered with a warmth and an élan that puts everyone at ease right away. Meeting him in this way, when crossing paths here and there, professionally, privately, or at social events, could give the impression of a form of intimacy. But it's misleading: while Sozzi does enjoy entertaining, opening his doors, and interacting with others, he is little inclined to share familiar or familial confidences, preferring to regale his guests with personal anecdotes about his work, travels, and hobbies.

To get to know him, one must follow him, which is no easy task. Sozzi is a mercurial figure, always on the move, leaving in his wake the subtle whiff of his distinctive cologne and a sort of vibration, a presence. It can seem as though he is right there, even when he's already off to the other side of his house, his office, his workshops or atelier. Or he's gone. "Dov'è il Signor Romeo?" "Romeo, dove sei?" (Where is Mr. Romeo? Romeo, where are you?) The question can be heard a dozen, a hundred times every day. His assistant, his sons, his press agent, his studio, his workshops: everyone wants him. To answer a question, solve a problem, make a decision. He never stays still. Always in the wind, as the expression goes—a will-o'-the-wisp,

[p. 215] ⟶

Typically Italian, relatively rare but proudly borne, the Christian name Romeo was popularized in the Middle Ages, derived from the Greek *Rhomaios*, meaning "native of Rome" and spelled *Romaeus*. Later the name was used to designate pilgrims who had been to Rome. *Buon Romeo* became *Borromeo*, and finally the "good Roman" ended up in Verona as a character invented by Shakespeare, age sixteen, family name *Montague* (or *Montecchi* in Italian). Meanwhile, San Romeo, celebrated on February 25, reminds Catholics of a canonized Romeo from the fifteenth century, a Carmelite monk from Lucca, in Tuscany.

Completed in 1596, *The Most Excellent and Lamentable Tragedie of Romeo and Juliet* remains one of William Shakespeare's best-known plays. Even though the lovers of Verona appeared in Dante's *Divine Comedy* nearly three centuries earlier, it was Shakespeare who made them a universal myth. A myth so strong, so enduring that it continues to inspire playwrights, filmmakers, choreographers, and composers to this day. After centuries of theatrical incarnations, Romeo and Juliet became a recurring theme in cinema starting in 1900. Prior to the advent of the "talkies," there were dozens of French, American, British, and Italian silent productions, most starring Romeos who were either too old or too fat, never believable and almost never Italian. In 1916, aspiring to celebrate the 300th anniversary of Shakespeare's death, Hollywood offered up its vision of the story with, in the male lead, the distinct-

ly athletic Francis X. Bushman, a natural-born matinee idol and future cinematic Ben Hur (1925). It wasn't until 1936 that the film world attempted a more serious treatment of the drama, aided by the invention of the soundtrack. The elegant George Cukor was tapped to direct a *Romeo and Juliet* that was, for once, faithfully and lavishly modeled on the play. Except that Romeo was portrayed by the oh-so-British Leslie Howard, who was, once again, too old for the part—*forty-three*—and radiated all the charisma of a doorknob.

After World War II, the tragic classic was given a British adaptation that earned great acclaim: filmed in 1954 on location in Verona by the Italian director Renato Castellani, in English and in color, with costumes by Leonor Fini, this version at last featured a Romeo of (nearly) the right age, the Lithuanian-born Laurence Harvey, and carried off the Golden Lion at that year's Venice Film Festival. Fourteen years later, Franco Zeffirelli scored a triumph with a *Romeo e Giulietta* that instantly assumed a prominent place in film history. Showered with Oscars, the film was a masterpiece, with, for the first time, teenage actors in the title roles: seventeen-year-old Leonard Whiting—the director's second choice, after Beatle Paul McCartney—as Romeo and Olivia Hussey, an Argentinean-born beauty, only fifteen at the time, as Juliet. Zeffirelli shot scenes on location in Siena, Gubbio, and Artena, but none in Verona. Of course, not all filmmakers have adhered so closely to the Shakespearean original: the mythical couple has been the subject of an avalanche of parodies, spoofs, and takeoffs, plus reinterpretations like *Les Amants de Vérone* (André Cayatte, 1949) with Anouk Aimée and Serge Reggiani. In 1996, Australian director Baz Luhrmann's subversive modernization, *Romeo + Juliet*, launched the careers of Leonardo DiCaprio and Claire Danes. More recently, at Cinecittà in February 2012, Carlo Carlei directed yet another film version of the play, starring Hailee Steinfeld and Douglas Booth, produced by Gabriele Muccino, with costumes by the quadruple-Oscar-winning designer Milena Canonero. Romeo and Juliet have also been depicted in comic strips, animation, video, and, before all that, paintings by artists such as Francesco Hayez, Joseph Wright of Derby, Frank Dicksee, and Pino Casarini. Not surprisingly, opera, dance, and musical comedy have also appropriated the mythology of the star-crossed lovers: Berlioz's *symphonie dramatique*, completed in 1839, operas by Bellini and Gounod; Prokofiev's ballet has not only been staged but also filmed, including notable Russian renditions. But the best screen version of his *Romeo and Juliet* was created by the well-known Austro-Hungarian director Paul Czinner, who emigrated to Britain in 1933. His last film, made in 1966, was an adaptation by the Royal Ballet with Rudolf Nureyev and Margot Fonteyn. In popular music, the lovely Londoner Petula Clark crooned a syrupy *Romeo* (or, rather, *Ro-mee-ohhh*) in the early sixties that put her on the international pop map. But the crown for the most parabolic, tragic reference goes to Jean-Luc Godard for a scene in *Le Mépris*, based on the novel by Alberto Moravia, in which Brigitte Bardot says, "Remonte dans ton Alfa, Romeo" ("Get in your Alfa, Romeo") just before the fatal accident. The Alfa in question was a Giulietta Spider; and Romeo, the American actor Jack Palance.

forever elusively aglow. But don't think for a minute that he's avoiding his duties and responsibilities: the human dynamo has already answered the question, solved the problem, and decided what to do next. At the same time, he's plotting out a new project, or, accompanied by one of his trusted craftsmen, arriving at the workshop at dawn to modify one detail and add another, acting on an idea that came to him overnight.

And don't think for a second that he is resting on his laurels, however deserved they may be. Sozzi is perfectly capable of leaving Milan at noon or Varenna at daybreak to keep an appointment Saturday morning or Sunday afternoon with a client who has come from far away to see him, and who a few hours later will be en route to another far-flung destination. Which is exactly what Sozzi does himself when he's in Paris, London, New York, or Moscow. It's easy to see how he has built up an exacting, erudite clientele, hungry for his made-to-measure creations, his top-quality workmanship, and above all his personal attention. The source of his fabulous popularity is summed up in a nickname: "Romeo Sozzi, the couture furniture maker." Still, he prefers to keep a low profile. Sozzi is not the type to brag or show off. And his humility is not a tactic—it's his natural disposition, especially when facing a challenge. "There's always something to learn from someone who does things better," he says. But this humble attitude does not prevent him from being amused by his other nickname, "Romeoccentric," in reference to his taste for the exceptional and the extraordinary.

Sozzi, who is originally from Valmadrera, calls himself a *laghé*—a man of the lake. Lake Lecco. Not because he rose from its depths like a mythological merman, but for having grown up by, and on, the water: Valmadrera lies on the western shore, across from Lecco. Many view the lake-centered life as another state of being, another form of civilization. A laghé can leave the region and return, but never forgets his innate difference, his earthiness. Romeo Sozzi knows and says that he is different. He has his feet on the ground—and his head in the stars. A close examination of this particular *laghé* reveals a man of two essences, an oxymoronic duality. On one side, the rugged, mineral immutability of the mountains, and on the other a tremendous open-mindedness, luminosity, and fluidity derived from the lake. The *laghé* is by nature both inflexible and atavistically creative. Although fastidious, or even stubborn, it's always for a reason. Tenacious in his work, never wavering from his path, with the persistence of one possessed. A maniac steeped in common sense but eager to outdo himself. Knowing himself well, he even offers a few hints, reveals a few keys to his personality, with his customary nonchalance. A remarkable man who knows how to make himself unforgettable.

Romeo Sozzi was born in Valmadrera in 1948. His father, Felice, was a man of the lake and of wood, the owner of a high-end carpenter's shop. His grandfather fit the tradition as well, although on a more modest scale: *Nonno Sozzi* was a wheelwright who ran a small workshop in Valmadrera that produced handcrafted wagons, carts, and buggies, and repaired the carriages of the local aristocracy. Apprenticed at a very young age to a carpenter in Lecco, Felice Sozzi completed his professional training at the carpentry school in Cantù, a town near Como known as the cradle of Italian cabinetmaking. The first of the dynasty to embrace modernity, he became a cabinetmaker and returned to Lecco, where he opened a workshop under the name Sozzi Felice Arredamenti ("& Figli" would be added later). The quality of its workmanship soon drew the attention of accomplished designers like Gio Ponti, also trained in Cantù, who came to Lecco to work with the company. After that, the orders poured in from local interior designers hired to furnish and decorate the houses in the region, consolidating the house's reputation.

In his turn, Romeo Sozzi went off to study at the **Brera Academy,**[*] a prestigious art school in Milan. And in his turn he came back to Valmadrera to work in interior design. Married in 1972 and a father soon after, Sozzi started out selling fabrics by high-end brands like Sahco/Ulf Moritz, Fortuny, Larsen, and Sherri Donghia. He opened a showroom in the city center of Lecco.

In addition to fabrics, the sensuous foundation of his work, he soon branched out to contemporary furniture, selling pieces by De Padova, Knoll, Cassina, Thonet, and Bulthaup, as well as antiques selected for their beauty and elegance. His first such acquisition was an eighteenth-century commode, which he bought for 1.2 million lire, lovingly restored and then resold. Like his father, he built up an ever-widening reputation, which in his case extended far beyond the lake region: the first house that he decorated was for the shoe and leather goods maker Andrea Carrano. "Carrano lived in New York, where he had made a fortune—he had a

[p. 220] ⟶

◆ THE ACCADEMIA DI BRERA:
A MILANESE MONUMENT TO THE ARTS

In addition to commissioning La Scala, Empress Maria-Theresa of Austria was the force who founded the Brera Academy of Fine Arts, which soon built a reputation as one of Europe's finest training centers for art and music. Although its school of architecture split off to join the coterie of the Politecnico di Milano in the late nineteenth century, at the same time Brera's school of sculpture entered a golden age under the strict supervision of the renowned Adolfo Wildt, and later, Marino Marini. The future alumni included Lucio Fontana and Fausto Melotti. Through its presence and prestige, the Accademia established Brera as the bohemian neighborhood of Milan. The Pinacoteca, now an independent public gallery, was originally used for didactic exhibitions of the art students' works. Its new design, created by the filmmaker and scenographer Ermanno Olmi, director of *The Tree of Wooden Clogs*, offers an ideal setting for priceless treasures like *Supper at Emmaus* by Caravaggio, *Lamentation over the Dead Christ* by Mantegna and Giovanni Bellini's *Pietà*, plus many other masterpieces by the likes of Rubens, Van Dyck, Rembrandt, Guido Reni, Boccioni, Modigliani, Morandi.

The Accademia di Brera's sphere of influence extends all the way to Lake Como, specifically to Isola Comacina, an eighteen-acre island bequeathed to the academy by Albert I of Belgium. A plan to build an artists' colony there, with a hotel, villas, and studios, was developed in the 1930s by the architect Pietro Lingeri but never completed.

LECCO,
THE OTHER CITY ON THE LAKE

On the map, Lecco is at about the same latitude as Como. But the two "capitals" of the lake are worlds apart, separated, for one thing, by a mountainous isthmus, a delta of rock separating Lake Lecco from Lake Como. Their climates are also different, as well as their histories: for many years, Lecco was allied with Milan in the war that pitted the duchy against Como and Lugano. Located on the eastern shore of Lake Lecco, itself the eastern branch of Lake Como, dominated by the towering Monte Resegone, the city-province of Lecco is an elegant lakeside town under the spiritual protection of San Nicolo, represented by a gilded statue on a pedestal rising out of the lake. Having been controlled by the Viscontis, the Spanish, the Austrians, Napoleon, the Russians, the French again, and the Austrians once more, Lecco was the birthplace of many future patriots who fought under Garibaldi. Its history can be traced in the many monuments, churches, palaces, villas, and museums that grace the town today, including a Galleria Comunale d'Arte.

Against a backdrop of mountain climbing, regattas, and the annual *Carnevale*, the Lecchese (pronounced *leh-KEH-zay*) venerate the poet and novelist Alessandro Manzoni, a native son and a hero of Italian letters, nearly forgetting that Stendhal produced more works—both in quantity and quality—that were set in their city. An industrial town that made the transition from steelworks to electrical plants and then to construction and tourism, Lecco is proud to have housed, in the early nineteenth century, the recruitment center for the Vatican's Swiss Guards, and to have been, in 1837, the first city in Italy to install oil streetlamps. Lecco is also where the Dodesini brothers developed and patented their *fantasmini*, the well-known, low-cut socks designed to be worn in the summer with lightweight shoes, loafers, and sneakers but not seen (hence the name, which means *little ghosts*). It is a seemingly trivial invention that has nonetheless won the hearts and soles of millions of Italians. Lastly, Lecco is home to a branch of the Politecnico di Milano, a well-respected university of architecture, engineering, and design. The heritage of the designer and architect Ico Parisi, the architect Giacomo "Mino" Fiocchi, a Lecco native who also worked in his hometown, and the true-blue *Lecchese* Walter De Silva, star designer of Alfa Romeo and VW, seems assured.

Rolls Royce Silver Cloud II with the license plate A1," Sozzi recalls. "He bought a former abbey on Long Island, and that was my debut décor." That project was followed by a commission in Lecco for the apartment of a cousin by marriage, for whom Sozzi installed a spacious kitchen with a waxed natural oak parquet floor. Meanwhile, he had begun designing furniture and enjoyed a degree of success. Starting from his first project, completed on his own when he was just twenty four years old, he made continuous progress, developing his style, and refining his aesthetic signature. Not one to shy away from work, Sozzi is a firm believer in the principle of "try, try again," never giving up anything—especially not the feel of wood.

Sozzi eventually shortened the name of the family firm from Sozzi Felice Arredamenti & Figli to Sozzi Arredamenti. Headquarters: Valmadrera. Showroom: **Lecco.**˙ The 37-year-old Sozzi had the date engraved in marble: April 19, 1985. The other "son" was actually a daughter, Giuditta, who had already left to found the lamp company È Luce. She did not venture far from the nest, however: her company is also in Valmadrera, practically next door to her brother's.

Three years later, Sozzi took a giant step forward by founding a cabinetmaking firm. He had no trouble choosing the name: **Promemoria.**˙ Not merely a reminder, but memory. For memory and in memories, with Latin for its historical roots. Romeo Sozzi worked furiously, doing everything, everywhere at once. The mountain and the lake; the *laghé* who became a powerhouse. The first client to knock on Promemoria's door was a collector from Zurich who had drawn attention at a Christie's auction, where he sold a 300-piece solid silver and ebony Puiforcat table service that Bill Gates snatched up for the not-at-all-modest sum of 3.5 million dollars. He had come to ask Sozzi to decorate his Manhattan apartment. Without closing the showroom in Lecco—which of course adopted the Promemoria logo, and is still in operation, cultivated like a pet project—Sozzi opened his Milanese showroom on **Via Bagutta**˙ in 1992, in the heart of the Lombard capital's fashion quarter. In keeping with his usual practice, in order to provide the fastest possible service to his first customer, a foreign woman who lived at the Hotel Duca di Milano, he got on his motorcycle and raced like the Road Runner to the city, bearing the *Pierino* silver platters that she had spotted in the catalog. That clinched the

[p. 224] ⟶

◆ PROMEMORIA,
THE FINE ART OF CABINETMAKING

In 1988, Romeo Sozzi, having acquired a deep under-standing of wood and its aesthetic potential, founded the contemporary cabinetmaking company Promemoria, serving as its head designer and infusing every aspect of its production with his signature creative direction. He brings out the beauty of the woods that he uses with varnish, lacquer, and an elegant flair, combining the woods with lustrous metals, Murano glass, alabaster, velvet, leather, and shagreen. Chairs, tables, cabinets, buffets, creden-zas, beds, lamps—his repertoire is refined and heightened by a sublime sense of color. Combining tradition with unconstrained creativity, not to mention the peerless craftsmanship that has made the brand world-famous, Promemoria carries out 90 percent of its production (with rare exceptions, usually involving rare materials) at the Valmadrera site, a 215,000 sq ft complex that houses the workshops (wood, leather, upholstery, lamps, finishing) as well as the design studio, showroom, stock reserves, and so forth. Behind its linear larchwood facade, the atelier now employs a total of 150 people—more than sev-en times its original staff of twenty. Some forty of them work in design, development, research, and graphic de-sign. Exporting 90 percent of its production around the globe, from Europe to the Middle East, from Asia to the Americas, Promemoria has showrooms in Milan, Paris, London, New York, and Moscow. Not long ago, Sozzi ushered Promemoria into the fertile lifestyle market by branching out to home fragrances, dining room accesso-ries, and fine porcelain table services.

In 2015, Sozzi acquired Bottega Ghianda, whose found-er, Pierluigi Ghianda, was known as "the poet of wood." A specialist in high-end cabinetmaking, now in Val-madrera, Ghianda has worked with the most respected international luxury houses and the top European de-signers, from Gae Aulenti to Cini Boeri, from Piero Cas-tiglioni to Gianfranco Frattini. Although Sozzi remains markedly reticent about this acquisition, his aspiration to live up to the late cabinetmaker's well-deserved renown reveals a distinctive facet of his character. His challenge will be to ensure the house's future without diminishing its indisputable excellence. Saved from dissolution, the Ghianda workshop will produce new collections of orig-inal creations by the world's most illustrious architects, under the artistic supervision of Michele De Lucchi, and based on a wide range of his inspirations such as sports, motorcycles, books, and photography.

deal, and word of mouth began to spread, lauding the designer, his brand, and his admirable people skills. The rest of the story is well-known: Promemoria grew, building its clientele, reputation, and prestige, opening showrooms in Paris, London, New York, and Moscow, and expanding from furniture design to architecture, with commissions in Russia, China, and the Americas.

Sozzi is the father of three sons. They all work with him, symbolizing the kind of Italian family tradition that commands respect around the world. The eldest, Stefano, directs the cabinetmaking workshops. Modest and retiring, he shuns the spotlight, only reluctantly posing for a family photo uniting three generations of Sozzis. Davide, an architect by training, heads the Interior Design Department. When he is not supervising a project out of town, or in another country, he spends his weekends tinkering with vintage motorcycles in the Valmadrera garage. Lastly, Paolo takes care of the finances and manages sales, research, production, and logistics. Four Sozzis in the boardroom, with one Romeo in the presidential seat: the patriarch's privilege.

While the public Sozzi admits to an instinctive love of color, houses flooded with light, and the heady scent of a wood-burning fireplace, the private Sozzi likes nothing better than to relax in a simply decorated space—even if it's the kind of simplicity that complicates everything, as Cocteau used to say. A bon vivant, hedonist, and dreamer, upbeat but with a hint of melancholy that he adroitly sidesteps with the elegance of a true gentleman, Romeo Sozzi seems to be carved from the knotty wood of the mountain forests that grow rooted in granite. A man of the city and a man of the lake, he is a gregarious host who enjoys puttering about alone.

On the weekend he rises early at 5:30 a.m., wolfs down a hearty breakfast, gets dressed, gathers his gear, and takes off for a hike in the mountains with his Lakeland Terrier named Gin. He takes a different trail every time, following his fancy and carrying across his shoulders a *zainetto*, a corduroy and leather knapsack. Inside he stuffs his driver's license, a cellphone for emergencies, a small Leica camera, a notebook, an A5-format sketchpad, a box of watercolors and a set of English water- colors found at **Sennelier**° in Paris.

From these excursions, every Saturday and Sunday when he's not out of town, Sozzi brings back ideas for photographs—leaves, tree bark, light—but rarely inspiration for décor or a piece of furniture. Is it compartmentalizing? His creative

[p. 226] ⟶

◆ VIA BAGUTTA, THE MOST MILANESE STREET IN MILAN

Parallel to Via Montenapoleone, and serving as a sort of luxury frontage road, Via Bagutta is the Milanese cousin of Rome's Via Margutta. A cobblestoned pedestrian street, it is best known to both locals and visitors as the home of Ristorante Bagutta, famous for its Tuscan cuisine and for being the city's only art gallery with a kitchen—the walls are lined with original paintings. The trattoria, now a protected cultural monument, was once a gathering place for Milan's artists and journalists, who made it their headquarters starting in 1924, and in 1927 began meeting there to choose the winner of a prestigious annual literary prize. Its neighbors on the street include perfume shops, jewelers, fashion boutiques, and the fashionable pizzeria Paper Moon. The famed Venetian shoe designer René Caovilla chose Via Bagutta as the venue for his Milanese salon. In 1993 Romeo Sozzi moved into number 13, installing a showroom that spills over to the upper floor and the garden in the back, connecting on the other side to 8 Via Montenapoleone: a courtyard for holding court.

◆ SENNELIER, THE COLOR OF ART IN PARIS

A historic purveyor of art supplies on Quai Voltaire, around the corner from Paris's famous Beaux-Arts school, Sennelier is a pilgrimage site for artists. The original shop, whose storefront has remained unchanged for more than a century, was founded in 1887 by Gustave Sennelier, a chemist by training with a fascination for color. He was an innovator, inventing new production processes, developing previously unavailable shades and perfecting the packing of pigments in a tube—a boon for landscape painters working outdoors. Not surprisingly, the Impressionists beat a path to his door, starting with Pissarro and Degas, and later Cézanne and Bonnard. Another generation, another genius: Pablo Picasso bought his paints *chez* Sennelier. The house also produced (and still produces) the highly prized *Bleu de Paris*, a blue powdered pigment used for porcelain. Whenever he's in Paris, Romeo Sozzi goes on frequent expeditions to the shop on Quai Voltaire, in particular to stockpile his beloved watercolors, before dropping by the many antique dealers in the neighborhood.

process is powered through other mental channels, including reading. An ardent bibliophile, he once founded a publishing house and printed his own books, giving them an extraordinary graphic presence. This venture lasted for a few years, and the effort didn't dampen his passion for books; books that he buys to give away as often as to read himself, fervently hoping that future generations will still love books as much as he does. For Sozzi, being surrounded by books is a need, designing a bookcase is a mission. And he would never put his books behind glass to protect them against dust. It's like parmesan on pasta: there is no greater travesty!

When he's not roaming the mountains, running between his atelier, workshops, and studio, riding or driving, Sozzi is still in motion, traveling the world, with Paris and London as preferred destinations. Wherever he goes, he searches antique shops, scours flea markets, and pillages bookstores.

A master in the consummate art of conviviality *all'italiana*, Sozzi is a living blend of nonchalance and intuitive, informal courtesy. It would be hard to find someone more likable, a quality that he achieves with no apparent effort. And it's infectious: his presence is disarming, inspiring others to reveal their true nature—as they get caught up in the vivacity that reveals the inveterate joker Sozzi must have been as a child—egged on by his twinkling eyes, their silent encouragement overscored by a pair of eloquent eyebrows. He is indefatigable, in high spirits, even in his sleep.

Sozzi likes people who make him laugh and whose critical mindset intrigues him. To converse with him is to pursue a line of thought that is constantly being broken off, restored, redirected, and reconnected. No nagging afterthoughts. No digressions. Just a patchwork of facts, places, people, and stories that lead to another, a new story studded with wordplay, sound effects, and evocative personal expressions. His favorite: *Cha-pe-au*. Derived from the French word for hat, as in "hats off" in homage—to a man, a woman, a brand, a design project, or a mirabelle pie (he loves those little yellow plums).

Another pet phrase: "We can put a man on the moon but we can't do that?" The *laghé* version of "There's no such thing as impossible." Equally expressive with his hands and eyes, he invites everyone in the room to come and look at something, a lovely pen in a display case, a nice slice of *lardo di Colonnata* on a platter, soundless-ly, like a lepidopterist who stalks objects and materials. Attentive to everyone, he

notices every detail about the people he meets: a scarf, a jewel, a handbag, a pen, a coinpurse…

In his eyes, everything has been said, everything has been done, everything has been written. Now it's all a question of culture, or the art of conceptualizing tradition, progress that has proven successful. "It's in the way you do things, reshuffling the cards to revitalize the game. But it has to be done with passion, enthusiasm, and a touch of irony."

Armed with his beloved pens and pencils, Romeo Sozzi does just that, moving ever forward. An impetus reflected in his signature, made up, depending on the point of view, of three letters, three sketches or three symbols: a lifeline, bursting with vitality.

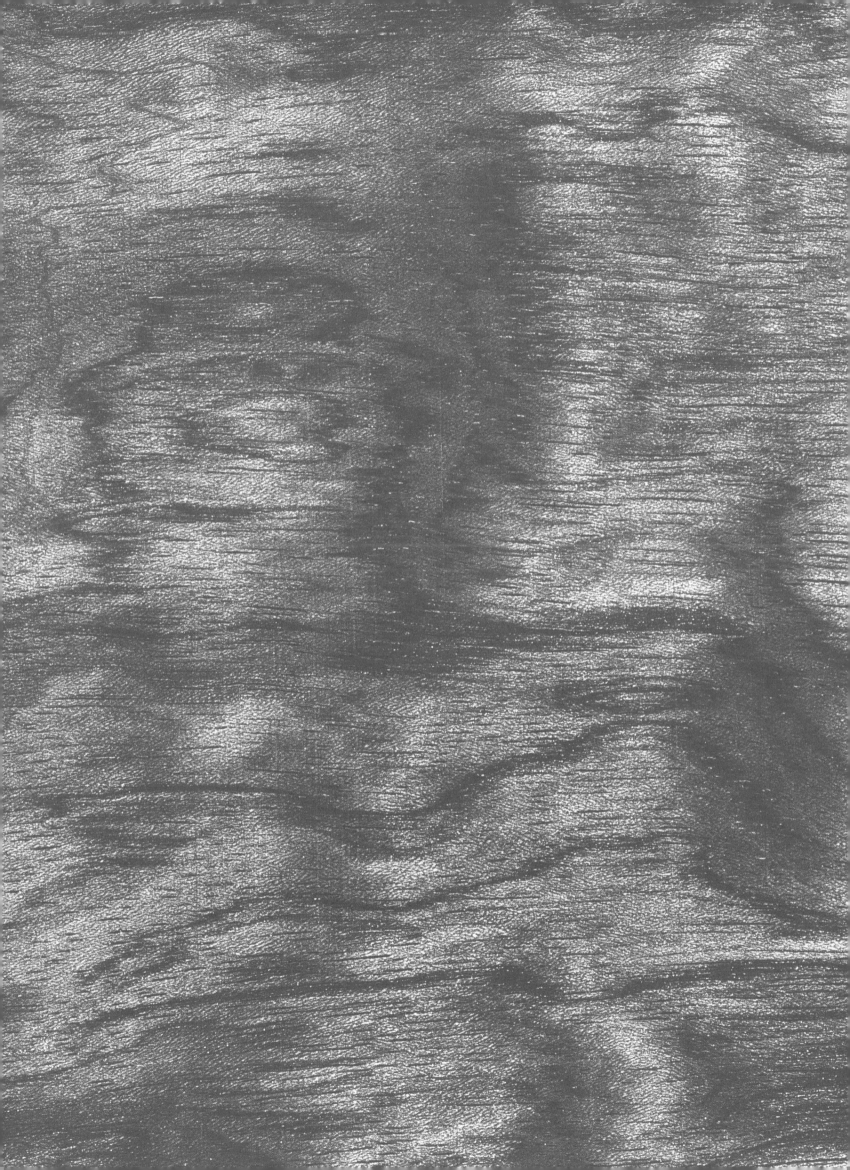

MEMORABILIA

ADRIANO. 2008.
Collection: Promemoria

Adriano is the modern Italian name for Hadrian, the Roman emperor known for his fascination with architecture. Many of the Renaissance *condottieri* (mercenary leaders) were named Adriano, along with numerous modern-day movie stars and pop singers.

Adriano is also a spreading, regal sofa with a Chesterfield-style tufted back and a velvety seat worthy of a throne. Its modular composition unites corner chair, *chauffeuse*, and *confidante* to reign supreme over the room, allowing its users to vary the methods of conversation.

AMARCORD. 1997.
Collection: Promemoria

Federico Fellini's *Amarcord* and his character La Gradisca earned the renowned filmmaker an Oscar for Best Foreign Film in 1975.

Such a statuette would look right at home on top or inside of this low modular cabinet, solidly ensconced on an extra-wide base.

Made of wood and bronze, versatile in both form and content, this *Amarcord* lends itself to multiple materials, taking on an aristocratic air in its "Halley" version with a gilded bronze base, ebony doors, embedded handles, and LED interior lighting.

AZIZA. 1994.
Collection: Promemoria

Languorous Orientalism in an opulent armchair tinged with art deco luxury, versatile with its choice of leather and textile coverings.

Decked out in cream-colored hemp or earthy brown hammered leather, two-tone like Fred Astaire's dancing shoes, with its own feet sporting antique beech, the *Aziza* amplifies its presence and volumes with a matching pouf. Steeped in sensuality.

BACCO. 2010.
Collection: Promemoria

An homage to Bacchus, the Roman god of libation, wine, and drunken revelry, this bar cabinet functions like a miniature mobile theater for the living room. Providing its own ultra-sophisticated stage set, it mixes cocktails as well as precious exotic woods—ebony, sucupira, larch—encasing a gleaming leather-lined interior configured to accommodate drawers, glasses, platters, a mini-fridge, and even a flat-screen TV. "Shaken, not stirred…"

BASSANO. 2008.
Collection: Promemoria

Jacopo dal Ponte, better known as Bassano, was a celebrated mannerist painter of the Venice School in the sixteenth century, the creator of masterpieces that are seen today in the world's most prestigious museums, including his *Last Supper* and *Supper at Emmaus*. At Promemoria, the *Bassano* collection encompasses dining room tables, coffee tables, and game tables that play according to the international rulebook, with precious retractable boards and pieces carved from ebony and maple for chess, backgammon, and dominos.

BATTIPANNI. 1999.
Collection: Romeo Sozzi

A tongue-in-cheek chair whose back reproduces in hammered bronze or rose gold the shape of a bygone icon of housekeeping: the old-fashioned wicker carpet beater. The *Battipanni* is an artist's chair that doesn't trip over the rug. With Empire green velvet or leather for the seat, it conveys a sense of humor and whimsy without sacrificing comfort.

BATTISTA. 1978.
Collection: Promemoria

A small, practical foldaway table in matte black lacquered wood, easy to pick up from its two-panel top lined with leather or shagreen, the *Battista* is, incidentally, Romeo Sozzi's first furniture design, dating from before the founding of Promemoria. Better than a bestseller, it's a "longseller," a signature piece now available in a full metal version in lacquered aluminum with perforated arabesques. The 2012 version in Bauhaus optical marquetry (maple, oak, and mahogany) has become a collector's item.

BILOU BILOU. 1999.
Collection: Promemoria

In the beginning was the Thonet No. 14, the most often used—and sold—chair in the world. More than 60 million have been produced so far. A pure product of the Industrial Revolution, universal and prototypical in every way, the Thonet bistro chair is above all a master-chair, a template that lends itself to any and all adaptations. Romeo Sozzi makes no secret of it: the *Bilou Bilou* dining room chair is quite simply his reinterpretation of the Thonet classic. An interplay of open and solid surfaces, produced in three sizes (standard, large, and kids), the *Bilou Bilou* has become an emblem for Promemoria, its beech frame adorned with custom-made velvet and elastic linen, and has even been re-created by some artists. Brash by nature, witty by nomenclature, the *Bilou Bilou* has risen to the status of talisman, a chair that gladly poses for the camera. It has even been the muse of the Milanese photographer Daniele Cortese, whose album *Bilou Bilou*, published by Promemoria, is a silent, eloquent almanac featuring the eponymous chair in a host of guises, shot with Polaroid, Lomography and Hasselblad. Everyone wonders: what does "Bilou Bilou" mean? The answer is: nothing—it's a nonsense phrase that started as a joke, an offhand fantasy.

CUBO. 2012.
Collection: Romeo Sozzi

Created with the goal of upending the accepted order in furniture, the *Cubo* is a three-dimensional paean inspired by the poetry of the right angle. An ingenious cabinetmaking *tour de force* in which functions collide, this protean, leather-strapped stool-cum-ottoman-cum-storage case is a pastiche of fine woods—ebony, palm wood, maple, and canalete—with bronze and mother-of-pearl trim. A pure, luxurious solid figure plotted with masculine irony, the Cubo is all about practical geometry: the perfect cube.

FOSCA. 2015.
Collection: Promemoria

In the early morning hours and at sundown, the mountains overlooking Lake Como take on romantic, evocative halos of mist that mute the natural light. An ebony totem rising from a bronze base, capped with a cloud-like shade in ecru silk, the *Fosca* floor lamp emits a fine-tuned light, subtle and atmospheric, in response to its touch dimming switch.

FROU FROU. 1997.
Collection: Promemoria

Frou Frou, or the suggestive promises of a dream bed whose padded headboard and voluptuous volutes conjure up black and white bedroom scenes from the platinum blonde bombshell comedies of Hollywood and the *telefono bianco* era of Italian cinema. Jean Harlow, Isa Miranda, Carole Lombard, and Silvana Pampanini all come to mind … glamour with oomph!

GEORGE. 2009.
Collection: Promemoria

When he purchased a villa on the shores of Lake Como, George Clooney opened up a veritable Pandora's box. Amused by the big to-do surrounding the film star, Romeo Sozzi decided to make a cabinet commensurate with his new neighbor's persona: huge, suave, and velvety smooth. The actor's wooden namesake is crafted from Tuscan cypress, with an LED-lit interior that can be customized in an unlimited range of materials. When closed, it looks as though it could serve as a confessional for hot gossip in the Church of the Sacred Heartthrobs. In fact, maybe it's actually named after Georg Gänswein, the papal *éminence grise* nicknamed the "George Clooney of the Vatican."

ISOTTA. 1976.
Collection: Romeo Sozzi

Isotta, or Isolde, is the heroine of an age-old Celtic legend, bound for eternity to her lover Tristan. It is also half of the name of a prestigious pre-war Italian automaker, Isotta Fraschini.

Since Romeo Sozzi never does anything halfway, his *Isotta*, a youthful creation but still as young as ever, comes comfortably padded with a unique contemporary look.

A bronze or nickel handle on the back, recalling the detailing of a classic luxury car, makes it easy to pull out. There's no such thing as paying too much attention to the comfort and convenience of one's guests at the table…

KETOJ. 2015.
Collection: Romeo Sozzi

A sculpture cast from molten bronze to evoke wood with all of its knots and veins, this trompe l'oeil side table/stool/bookcase comes in a limited edition of twenty five. A rare creation of extraordinary beauty, a covetable collector's item, the *Ketoj* (pronounced "Ketoy") propels the household object into the tracklit world of the art-design gallery. For those who were wondering, Ketoy is the name of an island in the Sea of Okhotsk.

MADAME A. 2003.
Collection: Promemoria

We know about Madame X, brought to life on the screen by Lana Turner, and "Madame de…" portrayed by Danielle Darrieux in the film by Max Ophuls. *Madame A* is a one-of-

a-kind beauty as well, ensconced serenely in Romeo Sozzi's apartment in Milan. A lady who came calling one day and never left.

MADEMOISELLE TECLA. 2014.
Collection: Romeo Sozzi

This precious curio(us) cabinet in ebony, inset with bronze stars and waves, owes its name to a fictional heroine. Signorina Tecla Manzi was the main character of an atmospheric novel of the same name published in 2004 by Andrea Vitali, a popular writer who happens to have been born on the shores of Lake Como, in Bellano.

Entirely handmade by special order in the Valmadrera workshops, in a limited series of twenty five, *Mademoiselle Tecla* is a lofty exercise in superlative cabinetmaking, sculpted from fine Macassar ebony and embellished inside with the customer's choice of wood marquetry, velvet, leather, silk or sheared fur.

MOKA & ROKA. 2008.
Collection: Promemoria

A dining duo inspired by classic bridge and cabriolet chairs, *Moka & Roka* can be distinguished by their details: the hammered bronze armrests, the open back… Two-tone outfits, wood and leather, witty and light on their feet — like Ginger and Fred, it takes two to tango, to have fun, to fall in love.

NICOLE. 1994.
Collection: Romeo Sozzi

Some furniture creations are clearly, proudly feminine. Dressers in particular, with their leather-lined drawers conceived to conceal lingerie, scarves, gloves, handkerchiefs, and accessories, are the very essence of intimate elegance. Entirely lined with parchment, the *Nicole* plays this delicate role to perfection. An exclusive jewel of a dresser, a gem in a chiseled maple setting, *Nicole* is pretty and she knows it.

STANLEY. 2008.
Collection: Promemoria

Originally conceived as an homage to Stanley Kubrick, this work-oriented storage cabinet has the physical presence of Stanley Kowalski in *A Streetcar Named Desire*, the size and the strength. A vertical volume in ebony with bronze details, the *Stanley* is as efficient and organized as any secretary, incorporating file holders, portfolios, document slots and a fold-down desk. With its doors closed, it also encloses a leather-lined stool. Dr. Strangelove would have loved it.

THEO. 1994.
Collection: Promemoria

Another famous Theo, the French painter Théodore Levigne, worked at an easel. For this *Theo* 2.0, the modern way to work is at a large classical desk updated with contemporary elegance. Five drawers, saddle-stitched leather lining, trunk handles or bronze pulls, a subtle mix of wood and hide, and luxurious and detailed treatments of fine materials ... More than just a desk, this is a grand arena for private interactions.

TORNASOLE. 2013.
Collection: Promemoria

Launched in 2013, the *Sun Tales* collection is a series of exceptional pieces, including this fabulous sunflower radiating from a central stem, with a round top that reinvents the typically Italian art of intarsia. Made for the dining room, emitting rays from its circular center like a mysterious sundial, the *Tornasole* cools down by switching from wood to white Carrara marble or onyx. Dazzling—and decidedly a conversation piece.

VITTORIA. 2014.
Collection: Promemoria

The ghost of Queen Victoria in a cushiony, futuristic armchair—a new rank of nobility for the bridge chair as seen by Promemoria. After scoring an imperial success, the *Vittoria* entered the workplace with an office version, angle- and height-adjustable, with a leather or fabric seat and a rolling bronze base. From regal monarch to working girl…

WANDA. 1993.
Collection: Promemoria

Wanda Osiris was a diva of the music hall, a musical comedy headliner, Italy's first gay idol, the star of song-and-dance extravaganzas on stages filled with staircases and chorus boys. Her life was a storybook and her career a whirlwind of success. When he discovered this sofa designed and produced by his team, Romeo Sozzi could only think of one name: Wanda! Sumptuous, voluptuous, delectably soft, replete with pillows, it's a medley of superlatives. *Wandissima*!

THANKS:

Maestro José Carreras
Mikyung Chung
Chiara Del Vecchio
Margherita Galli
Christian Kaufmann
Anna Liambo
Sabrina Mauri
Maurizio Michelini
The Sozzi family
The Promemoria team

PICTURE CREDITS:

Piers Allardyce: 140.

Richard Alcock - Gilles Charles Dallière: 8-9, 13, 17,
32 top left and right, 33, 36, 37, 38, 43, 44, 47.

Pietro Bianchi, www.pietrobianchi.com: 162-163, 164, 165, 166,
168-169, 170, 171, 172.

© Daniele Cortese: cover, 1st insert, 14, 18, 30-31, 40-41, 48, 50-51, 52, 54-55,
56-57, 61, 62-63, 65, 82-83, 84-85, 86-87, 96-97, 100-101, 102, 103,
104, 106, 112-113, 116-117, 118, 120-121, 4th insert, 123, 124, 126-127, 131,
132, 133, 134-135, 136, 138-139, 142, 144-145, 147, 148, 151, 152-153, 154-155,
156-157, 158, 160-161, 175, 176-177, 179, 180-181, 182, 184-185, 6th insert,
187, 188, 190, 191, 194, 195, 196-197, 198, 201, 202, 203, 206, 214, 219, 222-223,
227, 232, 8 unnumbered pages at the end.

Mario De Biasi: from the book *Espressioni*: back of the jacket, 39, 95, 110, 111,
119, 143, 183, 207, 233; from the book *Metamorfosi*: 107.

© Fréderic Ducout: 29, 32 bottom, 66-67, 71, 213.

© 2013 Piero Gemelli: 2nd insert, 74, 75, 76, 77, 78, 80.

Beppe Giacobbe: 99.

Silke Lauffs: 8 beginning unnumbered pages.

Jo Pauwels/© Beta-Plus Publishing: jacket, 79, 89, 90-91, 92-93, 94.

Romeo Sozzi: 3rd insert, 199, 200, 7th insert, 228.

© The Studio, Lisboa/www.thestudiosite.com: 208-209, 230-231.

Thanks to Giancarlo Brembilla for kindly having made available the vintage
postcards printed on pages 20 and 24.

*The publisher remains at the disposal of claimants
for any sources not identified.*

ROMEO SOZZI
& PROMEMORIA

THE DESIGNER BEHIND
THE MOST BEAUTIFUL FURNITURE
IN THE WORLD

EDITED BY
Pierre Léonforte

TRANSLATION
Anna Albano, David Jaggard, Sylvia Notini

ART DIRECTION
Massimo Pitis

GRAPHIC DESIGN
Gian Maria Fattore

EDITOR
Cristina Sartori

EDITORIAL COORDINATION
Laura De Tomasi

COPY EDITING
Chiara Ratti

TECHNICAL COORDINATION
Sergio Daniotti, Sara Saettone

First published in the United States of America in 2016 by
Rizzoli International Publications, Inc.
300 Park Avenue South
New York, NY 10010
www.rizzoliusa.com

Originally published in Italian in 2016 by
RCS Libri S.p.A.
© 2016 RCS Libri Spa, Milan

2016 2017 2018 2019 / 10 9 8 7 6 5 4 3 2 1

ISBN: 978-0-8478-4909-3

Library of Congress Control Number: 2015956202

Printed in March 2016 by Graphicom, Italy.